The Human Nature
of Learning

SRHE and Open University Press Imprint
General Editor: Heather Eggins

Current titles include:

Sir Christopher Ball and Heather Eggins: *Higher Education into the 1990s*
Ronald Barnett: *Improving Higher Education*
Ronald Barnett: *Learning to Effect*
Ronald Barnett: *The Idea of Higher Education*
Tony Becher: *Academic Tribes and Territories*
Tony Becher: *Governments and Professional Education*
Robert Bell and Malcolm Tight: *Open Universities: A British Tradition?*
Hazel Bines and David Watson: *Developing Professional Education*
David Boud *et al.*: *Using Experience for Learning*
John Earwaker: *Helping and Supporting Students*
Heather Eggins: *Restructuring Higher Education*
Roger Ellis: *Quality Assurance for University Teaching*
Gavin J. Fairbairn and Christopher Winch: *Reading, Writing and Reasoning: A Guide for Students*
Oliver Fulton: *Access and Institutional Change*
Diana Green: *What is Quality in Higher Education?*
Gunnar Handal and Per Lauvås: *Promoting Reflective Teaching*
Vivien Hodgson *et al.*: *Beyond Distance Teaching, Towards Open Learning*
Jill Johnes and Jim Taylor: *Performance Indicators in Higher Education*
Ian McNay: *Visions of Post-compulsory Education*
Robin Middlehurst: *Leading Academics*
Graeme Moodie: *Standards and Criteria in Higher Education*
Jennifer Nias: *The Human Nature of Learning: Selections from the Work of M.L.J. Abercrombie*
Gillian Pascall and Roger Cox: *Women Returning to Higher Education*
Kjell Raaheim *et al.*: *Helping Students to Learn*
John T.E. Richardson *et al.*: *Student Learning*
Tom Schuller: *The Future of Higher Education*
Geoffrey Squires: *First Degree*
Ted Tapper and Brian Salter: *Oxford, Cambridge and the Changing Idea of the University*
Kim Thomas: *Gender and Subject in Higher Education*
Malcolm Tight: *Higher Education: A Part-time Perspective*
David Warner and Gordon Kelly: *Managing Educational Property*
David Warner and Charles Leonard: *The Income Generation Handbook*
Susan Warner Weil and Ian McGill: *Making Sense of Experiential Learning*
David Watson: *Managing the Modular Course*
Sue Wheeler and Jan Birtle: *A Handbook for Personal Tutors*
Thomas G. Whiston and Roger L. Geiger: *Research and Higher Education*
Gareth Williams: *Changing Patterns of Finance in Higher Education*
John Wyatt: *Commitment to Higher Education*

The Human Nature of Learning

Selections from the Work of
M.L.J. Abercrombie

Edited by
Jennifer Nias

The Society for Research into Higher Education
& Open University Press

Published by SRHE and
Open University Press
Celtic Court
22 Ballmoor
Buckingham
MK18 1XW

and
1900 Frost Road, Suite 101
Bristol, PA 19007, USA

First Published 1993

A catalogue record of this book is available from the British Library

ISBN   0 335 09333 7 (pb)   0 335 09334 5 (hb)

Library of Congress Cataloging-in-Publication Data
Abercrombie, M.L.J. (Minnie Louie Johnson), 1909–1984.
   [Selections. 1993]
   The human nature of learning : selections from the work of M.L.J.
Abercrombie / edited by Jennifer Nias.
      p.   cm.
   Includes bibliographical references and index.
   ISBN   0-335-09334-5
   1. Abercrombie, M.L.J. (Minnie Louie Johnson), 1909–1984.
2. Teaching—methods. I. Nias, Jennifer. II. Title.
LB880.A357   1993
378.1'25—dc20   93–13277
                                                                                      CIP

Typeset by Graphicraft Typesetters Ltd, Hong Kong
Printed in Great Britain by
St Edmundsbury Press Ltd, Bury St Edmunds, Suffolk

This monograph is dedicated with affection and respect to the memory of Jane Abercrombie, with gratitude for all that I and others have learnt from her and for her skill as a teacher.

Contents

Acknowledgements

I am grateful to the following for permission to use extracts from the writings of M.L.J. Abercrombie (née M.L. Johnson):

Academic Medicine (formerly *Journal of Medical Education*), 1955, 30, 7, 381–91 (pp. 125–8);

Butterworth Heinemann, 1969, Gardiner, P., MacKeith, R. and Smith, V. (eds) *Aspects of Developmental and Paediatric Ophthalmology*, 15–24 (pp. 23–4);

Group Analysis International Panel and Correspondence, 1969, 1, 157–60 (pp. 98–101);

Health Education Journal, 1953, 11, 3, 112–17 (pp. 32–5, 47–8); 1955, 13, 1, 7–16 (pp. 29–31);

Society for Research into Higher Education, 1983, Collier, K.G. (ed.) *Management of Peer-group Learning: syndicate methods in higher education*, 100–4 (pp. 115–16);

Transactions of the Bartlett Society, 1965, 2, 53–82 (pp. 26–8, 41, 62);

Universities Quarterly, 1952, 6, 3, 290–5 (pp. 96–7); 1968, 22, 182–96 (pp. 60–1); 1973, 27, 465–74 (pp. 112–14).

Material has also been included from the following:

American Institute of Architects Journal, 1967, 48, 3, 89–92 (pp. 129–34);

Architects Journal, 1972, September, 581–2 (pp. 55–9);

Baben International Science Services, 1983, Tamil, P., Hofstein, A. and Ben-Peretz, M. (eds) *Preservice and Inservice Education of Science Teachers*, 101–4 (p. 102);

Contact, 1986, 91 (pp. 117–18);

Elsevier (Excerpta Medica), 1976, *Health Care in a Changing Setting: the UK experience*, 3–19 (pp. 52–4);

Group Analysis, 1985, 18, 1, 36–43 (pp. 165–8);

Journal of Architectural and Planning Research (formerly *Architectural Research and Teaching*), 1970, 1, 6–12 (pp. 135–43);

Journal of Architectural Education, 1977, 30, 4, 15–19 (pp. 144–52);
McGraw-Hill, 1972, Butcher, H. and Rudd, E. (eds) *Contemporary Problems in Higher Education*, 119–32 (pp. 123–4);
Medical World, 1958, July, 1–4 (pp. 49–51);
National Society for Art Education, 1967, *Journal of the Annual Conference*, 40–5 (p. 25);
Royal College of Physicians, 1961, Sandler, M. and MacKeith, R. (eds) *Psychosomatic Aspects of Paediatrics*, 146–8 (p. 38);
Society for Research into Higher Education, 1978, Abercrombie, M.L.J. and Terry, P.M., 1978, *Talking to Learn: improving teaching and learning in small groups* (pp. 103–11, 153–60); 1979, Abercrombie, M.L.J. and Terry, P.M., *Aims and Techniques of Group Teaching*, 4th edn (pp. 69–95).

While every attempt has been made to obtain copyright permission, it is regretted that in one or two instances books are now out of print and it has been impossible to make contact with authors, or journals have changed titles/publishers.

I would also like to thank Nick Abercrombie and Bill Lintott for their help and advice in selection and editing; and Rosemary West of the Rolle Faculty of Education, University of Plymouth, for skilfully tracing the sources from which these extracts are taken. Finally, without Caroline Bean's patient and painstaking typing this monograph would never have been completed.

Editor's notes

1. The conventions on the use of the personal pronoun have changed since M.L.J. Abercrombie undertook most of her writing. I have left the passages as she wrote them, knowing that her life and work stand as a testimony to the non-sexist nature of her thinking and behaviour. Nevertheless, I feel I must apologise to all readers who for 'he' must read 'she'.
2. When the author wrote as M.L.J. Abercrombie I have omitted her name from the titles of extracts. When she wrote as M.L. Johnson I have included her name.

Introduction

Jane Abercrombie (1909–1984) was a biologist who spent most of her professional life teaching medical, architectural and education students and university teachers who were interested in small-group discussion. The distinctive characteristic of her work was that it used group-analytic methods and principles in educational settings and to educational ends. Her aim was always to help students and teachers to perceive and think more clearly and, in their varied professional settings, to act more effectively. To these goals she brought the scientific rigour of her training as a zoologist, the insights she derived from working as a group member and co-therapist with the group analyst, S.H. Foulkes, and towards the end of her life with Cambridge Group Work, and her enthusiasm for and skill in teaching. Her research and writing continue to exert a significant and topical influence upon teachers in higher education, upon group analysts and upon students and teachers in occupations which require the ability to communicate sensitively and productively with others.

Her best-known publication is probably *The Anatomy of Judgement: an investigation into the processes of perception and reasoning* (1960; 1969; 1989). Most of her other writing, undertaken over fifty years, under the names of M.L. Johnson and M.L.J. Abercrombie, is scattered throughout a host of journals, conference proceedings, research papers and books. Some of it is out of print, and much is now hard to locate outside large academic libraries. These facts, together with the renewed interest within institutions of higher education in peer interaction and peer support for learning, in the pedagogical skill and quality of university teachers and their need for professional training, and the continuing demand by diverse occupational groups for courses in group work, have led the Society for Research into Higher Education to publish these selections from her work.

Jane Abercrombie (née M.L. Johnson) studied zoology at Birmingham University and was appointed in 1932 as a lecturer in the Zoology Department there. During the 1940s she became acting Head of Department, even though she was young, a woman and a mother. Her promotion was rapid, even under wartime conditions, and owed much to her outstanding gifts as a teacher. In 1946 she moved with her husband and colleague, Michael Abercrombie, to London where, after a brief spell as a science teacher in a secondary school, she worked until 1958 at University College, London (UCL). There, Professor J.Z. Young encouraged her research, funded in part by the Rockefeller Foundation, into the selection of preclinical medical students and into the new ways of teaching them that she developed, drawing upon her growing familiarity with group analysis. Her research became widely known and acclaimed, especially after the publication in 1960 of *The Anatomy of Judgement*. She then spent five years at the Paediatric Research Unit at Guy's Hospital, undertaking research into the perceptual disorders of children with cerebral palsy, before rejoining UCL in 1963 as Reader in Architectural Education at the Bartlett School of Architecture. In that post she carried out research, funded by the Leverhulme Trust and the Social Science Research Council, and supported by Professor Llewellyn-Davies, into the changes which were at the time being introduced into the selection and training of architects. Previously, architectural education had tended to be individualistic and arts-based; the changes with which Jane Abercrombie was associated moved it towards teamwork, physics and the social sciences. Her involvement in course design and evaluation and in teaching enabled her further to develop, with students and teachers, the educational uses of small-group discussion which she pioneered with medical students. Her work in architectural education led the University Grants Committee to ask her to undertake developmental research into small-group teaching in universities (1972–5) and this she did until she retired from the Bartlett School in 1975. From 1977 until 1980 she was funded by the Nuffield Foundation to monitor developments in new clinical courses for medical students, while based at the Radiology Department at Addenbrookes Hospital, Cambridge, where her family home now was. During the last years of her life, she took part in the planning and teaching of courses in educational management at the Cambridge Institute of Education, continuing the involvement with education students that had started in 1973 while she was a Visiting Professor at Sydney University, Australia. At various times, she also held this position in other universities in Australia, Canada and South Africa.

From the early 1950s onwards she also developed her interest in group analysis and was an active member of the Group Analytic Society. In 1981 she gave the annual S.H. Foulkes Lecture, entitled 'Beyond the unconscious – group analysis applied'. Just before her death in 1984 she had begun drafting the opening lecture, provocatively entitled 'Group analysis – a tool for the next biological revolution', for the Society's London Workshop. She was instrumental in the early 1980s in developing Cambridge Group Work's use of discussion groups in the teaching of group-analytic theory. From the 1960s onwards, she was also energetically involved with the Society for Research into Higher Education. Two of her major publications, *Aims and Techniques of Group Teaching* (Abercrombie, 1970; Abercrombie and Terry, 1979) and *Talking to Learn* (Abercrombie and Terry,

1978a), were published by SRHE. It is characteristic that when she died, aged 75, she was a vigorous and much respected participant in planning for two courses: one for the Group Analytic Society and one for the Cambridge Institute of Education. She died, as she lived, generously, joyously and enthusiastically involved in the development of the two concerns which she had spent most of her professional life bringing together.

Jane Abercrombie was a prolific writer. Altogether her publications number nearly 150 and have been translated into Czech, Spanish and Swedish. The earliest, published from 1934 onwards, are zoological. One of the last, given at a conference in Mexico City in 1983, is a typescript of an illustrated talk entitled 'Changing higher education by the application of some group-analytic ideas' (see pp. 9–18, 36–7, 39–40). During the intervening fifty years, she wrote many zoological papers, edited with her husband, Michael, the Penguin series *New Biology* (1945–60), and with M. Abercrombie and C.J. Hickman compiled *The Penguin Dictionary of Biology*, first issued in 1951 and revised for the fifth time in 1980. However, she also wrote articles, papers, books, chapters about science teaching at school and university; examinations and their role in the selection of medical and architectural students; the physiological, personal and social factors which influence perception, interpretation, reasoning and communication; the effect upon understanding and communication of words, visual images, spatial cues and context; the perceptual and visuomotor abilities and impairments of children with cerebral palsy; creativity and change; the purposes and uses of small groups in higher education; the education of students in higher education; the professional education of teachers in higher education; and the work of S.H. Foulkes and its application in higher education.

She was also a talented and sensitive face-to-face communicator who was often asked to contribute to conferences and in-service courses in many parts of the world. One of the decisions I faced as her editor was how far to alter the colloquial and even occasionally ungrammatical nature of her writing, when it was obviously printed verbatim from a lecture or discussion. Her success in personal communication depended in part upon her charm, informality and capacity to address her audiences in terms which they were likely to understand. In editing her spoken words, I have tried to preserve these qualities, while making minor changes which bring them more in line with the conventions of written English than they originally were.

Jane Abercrombie's success as a communicator also depended upon her awareness of the visual and of the power of the non-verbal. She was actively involved in producing videotapes for use in higher education (for example, on perception and communication and on small-group teaching). Her conference 'lectures' were often constructed around slides, pictures and visual effects (particularly the rotating trapezoid which was an essential part of her luggage on academic journeys). Many of her articles contain illustrations, diagrams and drawings. There are so many of these and the reproductive quality of the older ones is often so poor that I have reluctantly decided not to include any illustrative material in this book. My belief is that her words are more likely to convey the richness, variety and quality of her thinking if they stand alone on the page than they would if they were accompanied by a small, indistinct or unrepresentative selection of the visual elements of which her talks and writings were full. However, this is a great loss, particularly since her sources were startling in their variety and provocative in their juxtaposition. For example, some of the illustrations she used for her work on perception were: drawings of cave paintings, seventeenth-century etchings of French cathedrals, family photographs, early Picasso paintings, Rembrandt drawings, optical illusions, photographs of vintage cars and a ship's boiler, radiographs, medical photographs, children's drawings, illustrations from American experiments on spatial perception, labels from canned food, diagrams of the eye movements of experimental subjects copying geometric figures, photographs of village housing in South Africa. In the absence of such illustrations, I hope the reader will use the cues in the text to imagine the visual stimuli which existed in the original and which played such a central role in all her work.

Her extensive knowledge and her ability to synthesize and juxtapose the unexpected constantly surprise and delight the reader in the same way that her pictorial and spatial examples affected her listeners. Her eclecticism is not, however, an indication of random or disconnected interests. Rather, a number of interlocking themes run through her work; as she took up new posts and embarked upon fresh research projects, she build upon these key concerns, seeing and creating connections between things and ideas which to others often seemed discrete. It is these abiding enthusiasms which give her varied lectures and publications their sense of unity. So, for example, her interest in perception originated in her own training as a scientist, was stimulated by the difficulties of teaching zoology to school pupils and to university students, developed through five years of research into cerebral palsy, was given fresh impetus by the task of designing and teaching courses for architecture students, was strengthened and enriched by her long association with group analysis, and was nourished outside her work both by her experience as a mother and grandmother and by her interest in the visual arts.

The main themes which thread together fifty years of research and teaching are: the active and subjective nature of perception, reasoning and interpretation and thus of scientific activity; the influence of the unconscious upon these processes; the social nature of human life and learning; the difficulties that adults experience in changing and so in learning and the reasons why this is the case; the subtlety and complexity of communication; the obstacles that authority-dependence places in the way of learning; and the educational value of 'free', or 'associative', discussion among peers.

The choice of extracts from the work of M.L.J. Abercrombie has been determined by these themes, though some have been given greater emphasis than others. I have excluded her scientific papers and books, because of the likely readership of this monograph. Even so, it has not been easy to select, given her extensive knowledge, her wise insight into many issues and the wit and charm which flash through discussions of both the profound and the mundane. If I have failed to include extracts which others feel to be essential to an understanding of her educational thinking, I offer my apologies, accepting responsibility for the gaps which will inevitably exist when the work of one prolific communicator is compressed into a single monograph. Nor does the bibliography include all her published work. Like many busy academics, she often cannibalized her own work and full references might have been repetitious.

The extracts from her writings are arranged in four parts. Part 1 gives an overview, written by the author herself, of her educational convictions and of the development of her research and thinking. Part 2 focuses upon three issues with which she constantly wrestled: the nature of perception, reasoning and interpretation; the reasons why adults find it hard to change and to learn; and the factors involved in communication and the reasons why teachers and learners often fail to communicate effectively. The extracts in this part have been selected and juxtaposed with three purposes in mind: to emphasize each of these issues in turn; to show that she did not see them as discrete, but as continually interacting with and feeding into one another; and to illustrate the way she built upon her ideas, restating familiar claims in different ways, extending or presenting fresh facts or existing arguments or incorporating them into the development of new ones. Part Three examines the methods and principles of group analysis as she felt they could be applied in higher education and as she applied them in her own teaching. The long extract from *Aims and Techniques of Group Teaching* (1970) with which Part 3 begins is included in order to show the ways in which 'associative' groups differ from the teaching and learning groups more commonly used in higher education. This part also picks up the theme of authority-dependency and includes some of Abercrombie's writings on the role of the leader (or conductor) in small-group discussions. Part 4 gives detailed examples of the courses which she designed and taught as part of her research and in the light of the insights that she gained from it. These extracts are included for the benefit of readers who want further detail about her research and development methods or who seek practical suggestions to help in their own planning and teaching of courses which aim to encourage peer support and challenge through the use of small groups.

Two further points need to be made about the contents of this volume. First, I have not included any extracts from *The Anatomy of Judgement*, though I have drawn upon articles which describe and use this pioneer piece of research into medical education. There are two reasons for this omission: her book was reissued in 1989; and it is so well crafted that it would be difficult to take pieces from it without destroying its integrity. It is, however, essential reading for anyone with an interest in perception, in the nature of scientific thinking and activity or in the teaching of adults.

Second, the extracts have been selected and arranged to demonstrate the logical coherence as well as the divergence which characterize her thinking. However, because it was a deliberate part of Jane Abercrombie's pedagogy to challenge, puzzle and intrigue her listeners and readers, I have written a preface to each part of the book. In each preface I have set out a broad framework of the main relevant ideas so that readers may fit individual extracts into it or measure them against it.

Part 1

Overview: A Personal Account of Research into Higher Education

Preface

Towards the end of her life Jane Abercrombie was asked to speak at the Eighth International Conference of Group Psychotherapy, in Mexico City. She used this opportunity to review her research and her work as a teacher, to show how, for over forty years, each had enriched the other in her work, to demonstrate the importance to both of her continuing experience with the methods and principles of group analysis and to compare and contrast the purposes and techniques of teaching and psychotherapy. Her conference paper offers a cogent and considered account of her own academic and pedagogic development, as she saw them. I have taken from it extracts which summarize her career as a teacher and researcher, which set out her educational aims and convictions, and which explain why she felt that the work of the group analyst, S.H. Foulkes, had so much to offer students and teachers in higher education. These extracts give an overview of her career and her thinking, and therefore serve as a second, more personal, introduction. What is missing from Part 1, however, is the demonstration that she gave at the start of her lecture of some of the factors which habitually influence and distort human perception and reasoning. Readers cannot easily share the sense of shock and puzzled amusement felt by those who experienced these illustrations and stimuli and who listened to her exposition of them. The written word does not do justice to the vivid demonstration which she provided on this and many similar occasions of the unconscious processes which affect perception, of the emotional bases of learning and of the social context within which it takes place.

Research into Teaching and Learning

From 'Changing higher education by the application of some group-analytic ideas'. Paper given at the Eighth International Conference of Group Psychotherapy, Mexico City, April 1984.

As a teacher of zoology at Birmingham University I had begun to realize some of the difficulties of training students in scientific method: how to observe accurately and comprehensively and draw reasonable conclusions from what one sees; how to see differences and similarities between things, to classify, judge, test, predict and extrapolate validly; how to analyse and synthesize usefully. It was in those early days commonly assumed that these skills followed automatically from the absorption of the current body of scientific knowledge. But it became clear that it was much easier to teach a student the facts than to help him to think about them; it was easier to demonstrate to a student what you could see in a specimen than to help him to discover anything else, or to distinguish what he thought was there from what was really there. Teaching the content of the premedical biology course to medical students, whether it was the insides of earthworms, evidence for belief in the theory of evolution, or the life cycle of the malaria parasite, did not seem to be preparing them for the practice of diagnosis – for using knowledge to behave effectively towards something that was only partly familiar or perhaps quite new and unexpected. It seemed difficult to make use of other people's experience without being confined by it. The difficulties seemed to be connected with the student's perception of his own relationship to knowledge, through his relationship to teachers. It was the authority-dependency situation that needed to be modified. I had also become aware that our teaching was based on a false assumption, namely that the straightforward teaching of the established factual body of knowledge of science would train students in scientific ways of working, would help them to behave scientifically.

So I started to supplement lecturing with exercises in problem-solving, and small-group discussion, and to question the assumption that one teaches zoology best by focusing attention narrowly and accurately on zoological data, ignoring its personal and social interconnections. At that time teaching in the universities was of 'pure' zoology, completely cut off from the applied biological work going on in the research institutes (on pests or plant and animal nutrition, for example) . . .

But teaching less didactically was not easy either. In the postwar years in the Department of Anatomy at University College, London, some of our preclinical medical students were ex-service men who wanted to be taught as quickly and effortlessly as possible in the old-fashioned way. I complained to a colleague about the belligerent behaviour of an aggressive group of students, comparing it jokingly to what I had read of group psychotherapy, and he gave me an introduction to a friend who was conducting therapeutic groups of skin patients at the Middlesex Hospital. I dropped in on one of his sessions and realized that if I could produce for students the kind of social climate he had established for his patients, half of my troubles would be over. The doctor was a colleague of Dr S.H. Foulkes, and through him I joined one of Dr Foulkes's groups. I want to stress that it was the social climate, the 'group situation', that seemed important, even for an activity, learning to behave scientifically, that is usually regarded as rational, objective, emotion-free.

During this period, as I struggled with the problems of training medical students in scientific method, I started my first project. Professor J.Z. Young gave me freedom to develop a series of 'free group discussions' and to separate my subjects into experimental and control populations, in order to test the effect of such teaching. The students who had attended the discussions did better than those who had not in tests of observation – they tended to distinguish better between 'facts' (descriptive statements which can be checked by reference to the material) and 'inferences' (with which one works in diagnosis, going beyond the 'facts'); to make fewer false inferences; to consider alternative hypotheses more frequently; and to be less adversely 'set' in reaction to a stimulus pattern by previous experience of similar ones (James *et al.*, 1956).

The 'situation' which finally evolved (the project, financed partly by the Rockefeller Foundation, covered ten years) was as follows. The students met with me in groups of twelve for one and a half hours at weekly intervals, for a course of eight sessions. The theme of the course was introduced with a demonstration of the projective nature of perception, which leaned heavily on the transactional approach of Ames (1955). This served to emphasize personal involvement in any act of perception, the importance of the observer's basic unrecognized assumptions (expectations, attitudes or schemata) and the influence of contextual factors. The similarity of these processes in everyday life and in science was stressed.

The meetings were firmly structured in time and place. For twenty minutes or so the students worked individually at a scientific task, such as comparing and contrasting two radiographs, evaluating a published report or an experiment, or defining the word 'normal'. There followed free discussion about the individual responses to the task, in which the egocentric nature of perception became clear. Each person had responded idiosyncratically to the same stimulus pattern, according to his basic assumptions and reactions to contextual factors. By comparing and contrasting his own judgements and those of his peers he could become conscious of some of the multitude of interacting factors that had profoundly influenced him but of which he had been unaware. Whereas in the didactic situation he is offered the teacher's judgement, the authoritative correct one, with which to compare his own, in the group he is confronted with eleven others, made by his peers, which he must evaluate on their own merits.

In Foulkes's terminology, the groups could be described as short-term (eight weeks), closed (twelve students) and monosymptomatic (deficient in scientific objectivity). They were quite different from therapeutic groups in two ways. First, attention was focused on a particular topic by the initial exercise done individually. Second, the members were colleagues, not strangers to each other, and there could be no insistence on 'abstinence', no attempt to prevent meeting outside the group; on the contrary, discussion often continued both between members of the same group and with those in other groups. I felt this was an advantage, in encouraging the transfer of training beyond the group situation, and disseminating the ideas talked about within it into the rest of their learning. They resembled therapeutic groups in that discussion was *free* in the sense that there was no directive chairmanship; it was *associative* in that the perception of the relationship of seemingly irrelevant topics was encouraged, and *analytic* in that the attempt was made to clarify and specify the meanings of statements.

In conducting the group I tried to avoid being didactic, and to weaken the authority-dependency relation and encourage the strengthening of peer relationships. Undoubtedly I was perceived as an authority figure, as a professional scientist, as representing the department and the college, and as administrator of the course. I convened the groups, stated their purpose, fixed the time and place of meeting, arranged the programme of exercises, and opened and closed each session. I had the advantage, however, of not being an examiner; the course was optional, though there were few absentees. For the rest, I tried to establish a group situation conducive to learning through the sharing of experiences of the initial individual task. This involved making a supportive, non-threatening climate in which constant challenge to habitual ways of thinking was tolerable. I made few statements, and kept them very short; avoided breaking silences; listened hard and made use of what I had heard; encouraged contemplation and questioning. The project is reported in some detail in *The Anatomy of Judgement* (1960).

In the second project I worked (1958–75; see Abercrombie, 1974) in the Bartlett School of Architecture on selection and training, supported by the Leverhulme Trust Fund. The new Head of the School, Professor Llewellyn-Davies, was imaginatively concerned with the problems of teaching a new kind of architect, who could cope with the design of large complex buildings – hospitals, schools, airports, etc. – which required understanding not only of new building materials and technologies, but also of social problems of urbanization, leisure, changing populations and attitudes, changing needs and supplies.

This project took place in a very different setting from the first one. There had been widespread rethinking about architectural education and a thoroughly revised course was being implemented. Whereas with the medical project I focused effort on a small part of the course, and in some isolation from the rest of it, with the architects I was involved with the whole course as a kind of educational consultant, sitting in on classes and taking part in the many departmental discussions on curriculum and general teaching and examining problems. If the work in medical education had analogies with therapeutic groups, that with architectural education had analogies with therapeutic communities. Keeping in mind that students learn a great deal that is not deliberately taught, picking up habits and attitudes from the general climate or culture of the School, we aimed to make this as favourable as possible, trying to ensure that the symbols worked with us and not against us.

A major problem, as in any period of rapid change, was communication, and we attempted to improve this by many and various meetings for discussion. Discomfort and confusion followed the need for students and staff to accommodate to the continuing changes in role. The non-architectural teachers who came to teach subjects formerly covered by the studio staff brought the different attitudes and work methods of their own disciplines. It was not clear how these could usefully be integrated into design training. Practising architects found themselves teaching students whose knowledge in the new areas exceeded their own.

There was great scope for many different kinds of group work. The notion that an architect's work involves human relationships was firmly adopted, and we tried to make professional education the medium for good personal development. Task-oriented group work was organized in structures of varying sizes and constitutions – within the same year (sibling groups), and in a cross-section of the school (over five years) – to give experience of working with different levels of expertise, and for different aims – for collecting information, or for designing.

Free group discussion of current experiences of working in groups was encouraged. There were several cases of conflicting attitudes or ideas that it was necessary to come to terms with. For instance, the old conception of the architect as a 'prima donna' artist, and the belief that an aesthetically good design could not be made by a group, conflicted with the realistic need for team work in the design of complicated buildings like schools and hospitals. There was a need to identify with a master architect, and at the same time a need to be weaned away from authorities. There was a conflict between the effectiveness of competition in stimulating effort and the need for cooperation. Interchange of personal reactions to experiences was used to sharpen students' sensitivity to the physical and social environment, so that they could better appreciate people's needs, and understand how the things architects do to the environment will fulfil or frustrate the consumers' needs . . .

Towards the end of this generalized project a more intensive involvement with a particular class was undertaken, financed by the Social Science Research Council. This was with a new one-year postgraduate course leading to a Diploma in Architecture. The intention was to make a special attempt to educate for change and for autonomy in learning – to encourage students to take responsibility for their current education and to prepare to continue to learn throughout life. This involved a change in the authority-dependency relationship that characterizes our educational system, with far-reaching implications for changes in personal interaction between students and teachers. In order to facilitate the changes in attitude required, Paul Terry and I ran weekly groups with students and their tutors in which topics of current interest in the class work were spontaneously discussed. The problems of becoming less dependent on authoritative teachers were closely associated with those of becoming responsible designers and of adopting the professional status for which the Diploma qualified them. Among the themes that emerged were: the wish to remain dependent which conflicted with the wish and need to become self-reliant; feelings of impotence; discomfort due to the lack of perceived structure in the course; realistic fears of failure as a result of being independent and fantasy fears of reprisals from rejected authorities; resentment at feeling manipulated, and timidity in taking the initiative to manipulate; depression at feeling abandoned by tutors; exhilaration at feeling emancipated; recognition that one could have and use internalized as distinct from imposed values. These are closely interrelated with two other major themes we have studied, professionalism and the design process.

While the student's most clearly expressed fear was that of failing to learn and to qualify, the tutors' was that of becoming redundant in the new learning situation. It is not without significance that the course took place during the intense and world-wide phase of student revolt (1968–9). The course and some aspects of the group discussions have been reported in some detail (see, for example, Abercrombie *et al.*, 1970; 1972; Abercrombie and Terry, 1971; 1973; Abercrombie, 1967; 1974; 1977a).

For the third project (1972–5; see Abercrombie and Terry, 1978a; 1978b) I was invited by the University Grants Committee to try to improve small-group teaching in the universities. This project resulted from the great increase in small-group teaching that followed the expansion of tertiary education in the 1960s, and from the widespread dissatisfaction with didactic teaching methods. The difficulties that many teachers felt in conducting small-group classes successfully resulted from the fact that their own educational experience did not include group work, so they had no model to rely on, and behaved in seminars that were intended to encourage student interaction as they did in lectures, tutorials, and practical classes where more didactic methods are appropriate. My colleague, Paul Terry, and I therefore organized small groups for teachers to discuss their current work in small-group teaching. These were of the usual pattern, one and a half hours long at weekly intervals. Teachers from many disciplines and from different institutions came. As is to be expected in this relatively unstructured situation, discussion ranged widely, but could always be seen to be relevant to the academic situation the teachers might wish to use with their student groups. As conductors we strove to encourage interaction among the teachers, and to weaken dependence on ourselves as authority figures. In reporting their own experiences in group teaching and comparing and contrasting themselves with the others, each could get heightened awareness of his own behaviour as a teacher. Between meetings they could try out new ways of behaving in their classes, and report back for further discussion ...

Discussion in the group was reassuring at the personal level: it soon became clear that no one person's difficulties were peculiar to himself. These groups were also reassuring professionally because it became clear that the problems were related to general and fundamental aspects of higher education. As one member spoke of a recent happening and the others questioned and commented, it became clear that the incident described could only be understood within a complicated situation: the relation of the particular class to the rest of the institution, the personalities of the participants (students and teacher alike), their past and present educational experiences, their various immediate and long-term objectives. Slowly, the network of assumptions that each of us had relative to education and to personal relations in it began to become manifest, whereas usually we are quite unaware of them. Confronted with a wide range of alternative ideas and of ways of behaving to a specific event, one can recognize some parts of one's own idiosyncratic complex of assumptions and question their usefulness ... The wish to be liked was often expressed ... Confiding in each other in this way, they learnt to recognize the needs which lay behind their motivation for teaching, and could direct these feelings into more effective channels.

While the teachers were talking about their own behaviour as teachers, their position as learners in this group of peers meeting with a conductor was analogous to that of their students. An important part of the group work was taking advantage of this duality to help to get more empathy with students ... The conductor's withdrawal from the dominant authoritarian teaching role, designed to encourage interaction among the other participants, illustrated to the teacher how he could liberate his own students ... However, this comparatively non-dominating behaviour of the conductor was so alien to the image of the teacher that many on first experiencing it were disappointed that we did not go further into psychotherapy, nor use sensitivity training methods ...

Common to all three projects was the need to change the attitudes that gave rise to unwanted, unintended behaviour. In the project with medical students, the need was to change students' ideas about their relationship to knowledge and authority, to show them how intensively their own personal experiences affected the ways in which they learned facts and made judgements. In the second project, in the School of Architecture, it was to help students and staff to take a different view of their own boundaries, so that they could cooperate more easily in what is generally regarded as that most distinctively personal, individualistic process of designing. In the third, it was to help university teachers to change their role as didactic transmitters of bodies of knowledge to that of facilitating student autonomy in learning. Phrased in this way, perhaps it is easier to see the relationship of this kind of teaching to psychotherapy, since both require one's recognition of the mismatch between perception of the self in relation to other and one's effectiveness in life tasks, and consequent self-modification to get a better fit.

Teaching and psychotherapy

In trying to establish the value of group-analytic psychotherapy applied to the treatment of 'normal' people, I shall call on my experience of having worked with Dr S.H. Foulkes, first as a patient in a group, then as a therapist with him in groups of patients, and continuously as a colleague in the Group Analytic Society, London, from its foundation in 1952 to his death in 1974. This cannot be described as 'training' in group analysis. I think what I learnt, I learnt by incorporating aspects of Dr Foulkes's behaviour as a model for my own. One mopped up through the pores of the skin random relevant images of Foulkes's behaviour, ideas, attitudes. It all happened very slowly, though by no means effortlessly. It has left those of us who have had this experience expressing what we learnt in our own fields in very various and personal ways ... In my own work I have found it convenient to concentrate on the following aspects of Dr Foulkes's outlook and philosophy (Foulkes, 1975).

The first is the social nature of man. This is commonly ignored in higher education, emphasis being placed on individuality, focusing on the importance of making a distinctive, personal contribution to knowledge, etc. Academic work encourages isolation and competitiveness rather than cooperation.

It is only in relation to others that a person can get to know himself. Because each person has an individual physical constitution and a different stock of experience from that of every other, his perceptions are essentially egocentric ... Free or associative discussion is a useful way of enabling each individual to contrast his habitual ways of thinking and behaving with that of several others and change them if he thinks fit.

The second aspect is associative group discussion. By 'associative discussion' I mean that participants associate freely to each other's statements, nothing being regarded as irrelevant or meaningless. Foulkes encouraged his patients to talk freely about anything that came into their heads. But this did not mean that they talked at random. On the contrary, the network of statements that resulted from this 'free floating discussion' or 'free association' he regarded as expressing the communication of unconscious interrelations. The succession of these, and all the verbal and non-verbal communications made in meeting after meeting builds up to form the 'matrix' of the group, which he regarded as an important medium for therapeutic change.

In teaching, the conductor's main concern is to establish a climate in which free group association is possible. This he does by a naturally supporting and accepting attitude . . . everything said is worth listening to. He shows his own intense involvement and interest by his occasional explanatory contributions to the discussion. He picks out the themes, recalls past statements where relevant, compares and contrasts the attitudes of members where necessary. As the group progresses the other members will take on some of this work.

The main difference between the discussion for therapy and that for academic learning is in the topic, which varies with the specific task of the teaching group. In my first project, with medical students, they first worked individually at an exercise for ten to twenty minutes, before discussions started. However widely the discussion ranged, it was relevant to scientific ways of thinking and behaving. With students of architecture, the chosen topic was related to current goings-on in the school, discussion of design work, or examinations, or team work. In the university teachers' project, one member would start discussion by describing his recent experience of small-group tutoring, and others would chip in with questions or comments about their own experiences. Differences thus became clear between individual practices, according to departmental set-ups, or subjects, or personal styles. During the discussion the conductor would contribute from her own experience, not keeping herself apart from the group as in psychotherapy.

A further departure from the entirely free discussion technique suitable for therapy was made by introducing the courses with a demonstration of the processes involved in visual perception. The factors that affect the uptake of information visually can be used as an analogue of the receipt of any information. The demonstration included images illustrating the transactional, projective, interpretative nature of perception; the egocentric position of the perceiver; and the intrinsic difficulties of changing.

The third aspect of Dr Foulkes's work on which I have concentrated in my work is the context in which learning takes place. Consistent with his interest in the organism as a whole, Foulkes paid a lot of attention to the context in which any event occurs and its effects on people's behaviour. I suggest there is a tendency in education generally, and especially in higher and vocational education, to focus on a narrow field of knowledge at the cost of excluding not only other fields, but also 'personal' matters, and 'social' matters generally. The emphasis in teaching is on thought rather than feeling. However 'liberal' the old universities may have been in their monastic tradition of combining education with pastoral care, in the modern large universities students attend lectures and classes to mend their ignorance of the subject they have come to study, and in which alone they will be examined. They are children compared with the academic staff as far as specific knowledge is concerned. But in social, sporting and other 'leisure' pursuits they are regarded as grown up, organizing their 'own' time, managing their own societies. They are recognized by the state as old enough legitimately to produce children, to join the armed forces, or to vote for members of parliament.

The recent considerable expansion of counselling services in colleges and universities is insufficiently integrated with academic work to help with problems of the whole thinking man. In associative discussion, however, the boundaries naturally become blurred and the essential integration of the academic and the personal, of private and public matters, is permissively recognized. An example of this is shown by the reactions of medical students to one of the problems given in my first project. The individuals in the groups were invited to read a published report of an experiment which purported to demonstrate that excess of vitamin A in the diet caused diarrhoea in domestic animals. Each participant was asked to design an experiment on dogs to test the hypothesis. They showed very good knowledge of scientific method in the design of their experiments. But when I asked them what would be the outcome of their experiments, some thought the dogs would certainly get diarrhoea, many that they could not tell, and a few suggested the dogs might get constipated.

In discussion it turned out that a complex mass of interacting factors (basic assumptions) of which they had not been aware had influenced their evaluation of the published report. Most of these concerned their differing feelings about its author, rather than about her scientific data. 'Women can't do research' said one, but another countered 'Only very good women can get into research'; or 'Americans can't do research', 'but they're rich! Their laboratories are exceptionally well equipped'; or 'she worked in a department of genetics on a physiological subject', 'but genetics is a very rigorous, statistically oriented subject'. Some had thought that people can be trusted to have done sound work and to tell the truth about it, even if they write it up rather carelessly; others that one must be on one's guard against being taken in by slipshod workers, slack writers, or editors of journals who are not sufficiently critical.

Briefly, I like to think of this work in higher education simply as a further step in the same direction as Foulkes took in his own progress from psychoanalysis to group analysis. He wrote in one of his last papers (1975) that compared with the psychoanalyst in the two-person situation

> The conductor is not so much concerned with interpretation but with the uncovering of the unconscious part in the here and now of the therapeutic situation. We analyse the ego in action. We analyse the individual in the group in actual on-going behaviour and reaction.
>
> The most powerful factor in bringing about change and the possibility for further and future progress after the group has ended is based on this ego training in action and not so much on the insight and interpretation based on words as such as upon the on-going corrective interaction with others. This is the main spring of the mutative experience in group-analytic psychotherapy.

Corrective interaction with others is, I believe, also the main factor improving behaviour in academic matters. In associative discussion of academic matters students can see the comparisons and differences between themselves and others, recognize the different basic assumptions relevant to behaviour, and can change their own if they wish. The education group is not a group of strangers, as it is in strict group-analytic therapy. This, I think, is an advantage in the potentiality it gives for the direct transfer of what is learnt in the group to experience in practice, and for the strengthening and spreading of change in the work situation. And by no means should the conductor be a stranger to the group. On the contrary, I think one must be steeped in the educational micro-climate of the group, the department, the institution, should be aware of the conceptual and attitudinal problems of the discipline, and sensitive to the larger context of educational thought.

The differences in technique used by teacher and therapist derive from differences in aim. In education, by contrast with psychotherapy where the whole person is the target for help, we focus the attention of participants on specific aspects of their current academic work, and bring to light those processes of which they are unconscious. It is worth noting, however, that participants often reported peripheral changes in their own behaviour. Some medical students, for instance, said that the course influenced their general philosophy of life (one said, 'I can talk to the vicar now'); and some teachers reported that their lecturing improved, not only their small-group teaching, and that they got on better with their colleagues, not only with students.

I think in teaching it helps to behave in a socially acceptable manner and to avoid increasing students' anxiety above that inevitably induced by the profound changes in role, theirs and the teacher's. One must avoid the temptation to outsmart a student (which transference interpretations are prone to do) and in general be prepared to refrain from making a crucial point, because if you wait long enough the students will probably produce it themselves, a sign of increasing autonomy. At the same time, it is important to show signs of listening, learning and remembering, and to prepare yourself, when chaos seems overwhelming, or at any time when students ask for it, to describe the themes, and comment on the processes that have occurred. Teachers are prone to criticize this softly softly approach, but I believe there is enough anxiety in overcoming the natural resistance to change (Abercrombie 1976a), in the whole situation of being a student, of learning to become autonomous, and tolerant of ambiguity and doubt. In teaching, we recognize the tremendous power of the transference relation but we do not use its interpretation as the main medium for change. Rather, perhaps, we see it as an important and ever present constituent of the group situation which we engineer to encourage interaction among all members of the group.

Part 2

Perceiving, Changing and Communicating

Preface

Jane Abercrombie saw the three themes which form the focus of Part 2 – perception, change and communication – as central to teaching and learning. Of the three, perception was the fundamental one, permeating and sustaining the other two. It was also the earliest of her interests, stemming from the difficulties that she encountered when attempting to train zoology students in scientific method and, in particular, in accurate observation and open-minded, rational interpretation. All too often students, when faced with material of which they had some theoretical knowledge, found it hard to distinguish between what they saw and what they thought they ought to see. Furthermore, the deductions and inferences that they drew from their observations were affected not only by their existing knowledge but also by preconceptions and assumptions which often had no obvious relevance and of which they were in many instances unaware.

Her earliest major and best-known publication on the processes of perception and reasoning is *The Anatomy of Judgement* (1960; 1969; 1989). In this book, she describes in detail the experimental teaching which she undertook with medical students and the ways in which she found that their capacity to observe, absorb information and make and justify judgements was shaped by personal experiences and unconsciously held ideas and attitudes. This early interest in the active, selective and projective nature of perception was developed throughout the rest of her work, as many of the extracts in Part 2 make clear.

However, she was also concerned, especially in her research into children with cerebral palsy, with the physiology of perception and perceptual disorder and the relationship between motor abilities, cognitive abilities and the social conventions of verbal and non-verbal communication (for example, in maintaining or breaking eye contact). This research also led her into a more generalized interest in the perception and manipulation of spatial relationships, so that in her work with architecture students she was able to make telling use of her knowledge of the processes by which space is perceived, aesthetically appreciated and visually represented. She found three aspects of spatial perception and representation to be of particular value in her own course planning and teaching. All of them have some bearing on the relationship between individuals and the groups of which they are part, that is, on units and their components. They are: people's tendency to perceive wholes not parts; their resistance to analysing wholes; the influence upon perception and interpretation of the context within which perception occurs. Each of these aspects is discussed in one or more of the extracts in Part 2.

I have found it very difficult to select representative examples from her work on perception, because this theme recurs so frequently and in so many guises. In the end, I have been guided by the fact that this monograph is primarily intended to be of use to educators rather than to biologists or cognitive psychologists. Acknowledging that Jane Abercrombie made a wide, scholarly and informative contribution to the literature on perceptual disorders, through her research into cerebral palsy, I have omitted most of her writings on this subject, and have sought instead to illustrate the connections that she constantly drew between the complexities of perception and the tasks of teaching and learning.

I have placed those few extracts which draw upon her research into the physiological aspects of perception at the start of this part of the book, even though chronologically they come after her early work on observer error in science. The reason for this sequencing is the emphasis which she increasingly placed upon the unconscious and its influence upon perception, change and communication. Her belief in the importance of the irrational and emotional in teaching and learning acts as a thread which binds together the three main themes in Part 2. As editor, I felt that it was more important to stress this continuity than to preserve the chronological sequence of her writings.

It was only a few years after she had started to work as a teacher that she began to express concern about the role of prior knowledge in scientific learning. Its existence often served to inhibit fresh learning and so to retard change. At first, she focused upon consciously held information: 'It is clear . . . that, far from assisting in the development of the powers of observation, the possession of factual material tends to inhibit it. This, I believe, is not generally recognised' (Johnson, 1942: 57). However, from the 1950s onwards she became increasingly interested in the part played in interpretation and reasoning by the knowledge and attitudes unconsciously held by students. These, she believed, encouraged them to be selective and transformative in their learning, filtering what was presented to them and modifying it to suit their own ends. What individuals hear and see is shaped by their past experience. Conditioned by repeated consistencies in sensory or emotional input, they build up assumptions, expectancies or schemata with which they unconsciously and unquestioningly interpret and transform new experiences. The existence of these 'basic assumptions' shapes and limits people's ability to absorb new information, adopt different attitudes or behave in fresh ways, limitations which affect the flexibility of teachers just as much as they do the open-mindedness or responsiveness of students. By contrast, change becomes easier when people recognize their personal and social inheritance and so can begin to gain mastery over it.

The potentially inhibiting effect on individuals' learning of their assumptions was exacerbated, in her view, by the authoritarian nature of the educational system. The symbols and methods of traditional education, in schools and colleges and universities, encouraged among pupils and students dependent attitudes towards authority figures and the knowledge and attitudes which they transmitted. This 'authority-dependency' she held to be at the heart of the difficulties that many adults experienced in learning, for it prevented them from making independent judgements, reduced their capacity to make productive use of new information and inhibited creativity. Yet, she argued, often with compelling illustrations from, for instance, the work of well-known artists or technologists, innovators could not break with the past unless they were rooted in it. Creativity involved both understanding one's individual and cultural heritage and having the courage to destroy as well as to transcend it.

She also suggested that learning and innovation were intrinsically unsettling and full of challenge, and so were best undertaken in a social environment which gave security and emotional support, while fostering self-reliance and risk-taking. Change was necessarily attended by anxiety; learning had an emotional aspect which had to be recognized and accommodated if learning itself is not to be stultified and the opportunity of future change denied.

The third theme – communication – addressed in Part 2 is closely connected with both perception and change. It is also at the heart of the educational process. As a teacher, Jane Abercrombie was actively concerned with the technical aspects of communication (for example, seating arrangements in lecture halls and discussion groups; visibility; proximity) because she saw that they affected the individual's capacity accurately to transmit or receive information. But her interest did not stop there. In her explanations of the subject, she drew upon biology, psychology, child development and psychoanalysis, and she used as visual illustrations reproductions of Renaissance pictures, films of baby monkeys, pictures of suckling goats, children's drawings and other disparate material. She stressed four points in particular: the Piagetian notion of egocentricity (that is, it takes a child several years to develop the understanding that one's perception of the relationship of objects in space will vary with one's position in relation to them); the importance of visual, auditory and kinaesthetic cues; the central part played by the human face; and the impact of the physical, social and psycho-sociological context, that is, of the total situation within which communication takes place.

Extracts illustrating and elaborating these three themes are arranged in roughly the sequence in which I have described them. However, Jane Abercrombie was so wide-ranging and eclectic in her approach and so frequently brought together ideas from different aspects of her personal and professional experience that no absolute content distinctions are intended by the order in which passages appear.

The Physical Base of Perception

From 'Eye movements and perceptual development', in Gardiner, P., MacKeith, R. and Smith, V. (eds) *Aspects of Developmental and Paediatric Ophthalmology*, London: Heinemann Medical Books, 1969.

My interest in perception began with the problems of observer error in science and medicine. This did not seem to have much to do with eye movements. Such knowledge as I had of vision began and ended with the structure of the eye, an organ of dazzling beauty and numbing complexity. Its double origin as an out-pushing of the brain, meeting up with an in-pushing of the skin, is as good an example as any of the interaction of parts of an organism. But in describing the function of the eye, little use was made of the notion that it not only began but actually remained, even in the adult, in connection with the brain, and hence in connection with the whole organism. The relation of perception to personality was still not widely recognized. As to the eye muscles, these also were beautiful and elegant to dissect, but their apparently rational symmetry of arrangement was completely belied by their tortuous evolutionary origin. No fewer than three pairs of cranial nerves unfairly divided their services among them, and contemplation of this irregularity detracted attention from serious consideration of what use a living animal might make of them. Binocular vision and stereopsis were thought to be of some importance in the evolution of man, but many monocular people seemed to get by surprisingly well, having plenty of other clues to space perception.

It was not until I started to work on the disorders of space perception in cerebral palsied children that I began to take eye movements seriously. Nearly half of the cerebral palsied and other brain-injured children we were working with in a school for the physically handicapped, had squint (Abercrombie *et al.*, 1964). It seemed reasonable to study the version eye movements to see if they had escaped from the general disorders of movement from which the children suffered. It was possible that, just as cerebral palsied children tend to be retarded in walking and other motor skills, they might be retarded in attaining full development of control of version movements (even when there was no clinically obvious disorder) and that their delayed development of perceptual skills might be related to this . . .

There has recently been a great revival of interest in the importance of bodily movement generally for the development of visual perceptual skills. Kittens develop the ability to see better if they actively walk around than if they are passively pushed around, though exposed to the same visual environment. Men learn to adapt to distorting spectacles better if they are actively moving than if passively moving. The movements of the eyes are extremely important in many kinds of perception. If a person wears goggles with fields split vertically, half blue and half yellow, he will see the world blue when turning his eyes to the blue side, and yellow when turning to the yellow side. After some time he adapts to the coloured fields and sees the two sides both much greyer than before. If now the goggles are taken off, when he turns his eyes to what used to be the yellow side, he sees blue. One could say that he perceives colour with the movement of his eyes.

One of the most important functions of the eye muscles is in searching or exploring the field of vision to find important targets. Saccadic movements (those used in moving the eyes from one fixation point to another) are important in learning to perceive and differentiate shapes . . . to measure size and in copying shapes . . . Eye movements are also important in interpersonal communication . . . Argyle (1967) and his co-workers have studied the pattern of eye contact when people are engaging in normal conversation. They tend to look at each other in the eye, intermittently, the listener looking at the speaker more than vice versa. If A is talking to B, he ensures that B is listening to him by the number of glances he gives him; when he is about to start speaking, he looks away from B and when he wants B to speak, he gives B a more prolonged gaze. Although in normal social intercourse we are not very conscious of the importance of eye movements, we do understand them. We talk, for instance, about catching the chairman's eye, or making eyes at somebody. I have found it quite disconcerting sometimes to talk with a squinting cerebral palsied child because it is very difficult to engage him in normal eye contact. When one considers the importance of the mutual prolonged looking in the eyes of mother and baby, one realizes that from the earliest age difficulties of eye movement control may stand in the way of the child's developing normal communication . . .

To summarize, I want to emphasize the importance of eye movements in searching the visual field for the most significant targets; in identifying and analysing shapes, and therefore in helping one to represent them; in establishing non-verbal communication; and in helping to control verbal communication. A child whose eye movements are not so swift and sure as normal is handicapped in many aspects of development.

Analysis, Synthesis and Perceptual Disorders

From 'Perception and construction', *Journal of the National Society for Art Education Annual Conference*, 40–5, 1967.

Some spastic and other brain-injured children have great difficulty in drawing a diamond or a man, much greater difficulty than would be expected, taking their age and general intelligence into account. These were regarded as disorders of perception, specifically of space perception, but I believe they are more properly regarded as visuomotor or constructional difficulties – disorders of eye–hand coordination. A child who cannot copy a diamond can pick out diamonds in an array of different shapes. A child who copies a diamond made of matchsticks with a square, will tell you, if you copy her square with a diamond, that this is wrong; she can see differences, but not copy them. Brain-injured children do have perceptual difficulties (injury to the brain at any part seems to be associated with difficulties of figure-ground perception, for instance) but the difficulties that worry teachers seem to be due to construction rather than to perception.

In normal children, the ability to copy even simple figures lags well behind the ability to differentiate them. While still at scribbling stage, at three and a half years a child will make a different scribble when copying a cross than when copying a circle. At the age of five, a normal child can copy a square, at seven, a diamond. It is surprising that it takes two years, a quarter of his life till then, for a child who can copy a figure made of two vertical and two horizontal sides, to learn how to make one of four obliques . . . It seems that the child goes through a stage of finding it easy to represent his general idea of something that he is trying to represent. He will draw any closed figure – a circle, triangle, square or diamond – as a circle, and later he will add little appendages to indicate the corners. This means he has begun to analyse the figure, to study and to represent it bit by bit. This process ends in his being able to draw the lines of an angular figure separately, correctly adjusting their length and direction, and the size of the angles between them. He has learnt how to reconstitute the figure by correctly relating its parts to each other . . . There seems to be a general difficulty in development, and as a consequence of brain injury, of putting parts of things together.

Teaching the Perception of Space

From 'The nature and nurture of architects', *Transactions of the Bartlett Society*, 2, 53–82, 1965.

... I will try to be more explicit on one or two points about the education of architects ... A person can be intelligent in dealing with verbal matters and not very intelligent with space. Though even extreme adherents to the factorial view of the structure of the mind believe that intellectual factors can be developed, at least to some extent, by learning, it is clear that some people learn to manipulate space more easily than others even when given equal chances. There are reasons for thinking that differences between people in their ability to perceive and manipulate spatial relationships are partly constitutional, that is, fairly stable ... The strongest evidence comes from the effect of damage to certain parts of the brain which results in specific loss of spatial abilities, the verbal skills being far less disabled. For instance, a brain-damaged girl aged fifteen was quite unable to copy a pattern of match sticks in the form of a 'W', though she recognized that as the first letter of her surname (Abercrombie, 1964). The disparity between her ability to describe the shape and inability to make it is all the more remarkable when you remember that most of us find spatial relationships much easier to demonstrate than to describe verbally.

Now perception of space is very complicated. We use a multitude of clues to perceive the distance between things; the way they overlap or partly obscure each other, our knowledge of their size and shape, the perspective effect of parallel lines, the texture of repetitive patterns. All of these are especially well known to painters who can achieve extraordinary versimilitude of three-dimensionality in a two-dimensional picture. The architect has to deal with real space, however, not pictorial space, and this involves the perception not only of a visual pattern, but of differences of sound and even of temperature, humidity and smell. Above all, the perception of real space involves movement ... It is possible to show that various young mammals, as soon as they can move at all, respond to parallax, that is, the difference in extent of movement of the image of distant things compared with that of near things, when the head is moved. To this ability to estimate distance, they owe their safety on their first journeys from the cradle or nest. Later they learn to respond also to differences in apparent size of pattern due to differences in distance from the eye; this clue, unlike parallax, can be represented pictorially.

The topographic sense, the ability to find one's way around a building or town, depends on the ability to recall a succession of visual impressions in correct sequence, and relate these to recorded impressions of movements of the body. The ability to do this varies enormously; I am terribly bad at it, and several people I know who are as bad as me are women. Some men are fantastically good at it, being able to retrace a path walked or motored in strange countryside without having seemed to pay special attention to it. This again is not the same thing as being able to recall a static image, which I am quite good at. It is possible to visualize very precisely the position of a statement on a page of a book, but to have no idea at all of the position of the page in the book, that is, of its relation to a sequence. I suspect that kinaesthetic appreciation of space, the recording of impulses derived from the detectors of bodily movement – the labyrinth in the ear, the proprioceptors of muscles and joints – is of great importance to architects, and that its importance has been obscured by the dominant interest in pictorial space.

A further example is the perception of the vertical, which depends on the state of the body and is markedly affected by other sensory stimulation. In fact, we perceive spatial relations in the world outside with the whole of our body. We also perceive our body with clues derived from our spatial relations with the outside world. Openness or closeness of surrounding environment affects our perception of the size of our own head or length of our arm.

. . . It seems, then, that architects need to have their understanding of 'felt' space trained, as well as their visual sense. They need to become as aware of the clues derived from the movements of the eyeballs in their sockets, of the head on the neck, of turning to the right or to the left, as they are of the clues used to portray such two-dimensionality in drawing or to interpret it in photographs. This is especially important for getting the feel of enclosure; it is notable that the insides of buildings are much more difficult to represent pictorially than the outsides. Perhaps architects, as well as laymen, have been too interested in the static visual image of the outside of a building . . .

I want also to refer to analysis and synthesis, another topic which arises frequently when teachers of architecture talk together. It is widely thought that it is easier to teach people how to analyse that it is to teach them how to synthesize. This problem has caused severe heart-searchings at the Bartlett, because it raises the question as to whether the emphasis we have placed on the analytical scientific approach in the introduction to the course has exacerbated the difficulty that students have in putting the whole course together. The analysis–synthesis antithesis is an extremely complex problem which can be discussed at various levels. In the most general way, it is the problem we all have to face in getting any sort of work done that is not just the passive absorption of facts; the problem of overcoming natural laziness, fear of exposing our ineffectiveness, horror of recognizing that what we actually *produce* can never be so good and so beautiful as what we effortlessly dream about. I am sure the problem has to be dealt with at this level, low enough to be appropriate to the psychoanalyst's couch, but also in less basic terms. I shall use the response of children to a test of spatial relations as an analogue. In this test (an item in the Frostig Developmental Test of Visual Perception) children are asked to copy a line figure on a grid of dots onto an empty grid of dots. The more complicated patterns . . . can be done correctly by most children about eight years old. In younger children for whom the task is too difficult, however, two kinds of response may be given. In the first, the child tries to grasp the figure as a whole. One child said, 'Oh, it's a sort of eight', and drew a little figure up in the corner, hanging on to a dot, but bearing little relation to the grid of dots. The child does not bother to check back to the model and compare his drawing with it; he is quite happy with his intuitive grasp of the figure and with his construction of something which is more like the idea in his head than the pattern on the paper. At this stage he synthesizes, but does not analyse. At a second, later stage, the child really takes notice of the dot background with the stringent requirements of size, shape and position it imposes, and struggles to match his own product to the model, dot for dot and line for line . . . It is not, however, true to say, as one might be tempted to, that at this stage the child can analyse but not synthesize. It is because the child cannot analyse precisely enough that he cannot construct the figure correctly; he may start on the wrong dot, make a vertical instead of an oblique line, turn right instead of left. He cannot *construct* because he does not yet have a real grasp of structure based on analysis. Any one child passes through these stages with reference to any one figure, but the stage he is at depends on the complexity of the figure; thus the child who could only draw an '8' for the figure on a grid of 24 dots could make an accurate copy of a simple 'L' shape on a grid of 9 dots, though a year ago he made a little curved 'L' which, like the '8', was unrelated to the dots. Faced with the next most difficult task in the series, a complicated figure on a grid of 30 dots, he just gave up, but in a year's time he may be able to tackle it.

I suggest that it might be worth looking at students' problems of design in this sort of way – that there is a degree of complexity of task which they just cannot tackle realistically, though they could attempt it if they were permitted to do so intuitively, with non-realistic results. The failure is not, however, a failure to synthesize something which has been analysed; it is a failure to analyse, and analysis can only be achieved by the continued struggle to synthesize. We should not think of analysis preceding synthesis, but of each assisting the other. The implication of this way of thinking for the optimal temporal sequence of different parts of the course needs to be worked out . . .

Perception Involves Interpretation

From M.L. Johnson, 'Perception and interpretation', *Health Education Journal*, 13, 1, 7–16, 1955.

Perception involves interpretation, and some understanding of the factors influencing it may help us to present information visually in such a way that it will have for the recipient, as well as for ourselves, the meaning we wish to convey.

Consider briefly the anatomy and physiology of the perceptual process. What is it that the perceiver actually receives? Whatever is presented to him, whether a picture or a real three-dimensional object, it reaches him as a pattern of light and shade impinging on the eye. Of the thousands of minute receptors in the retina, some are stimulated and others not. After a series of relayings of impulses through the central nervous system by a network of pathways whose complexity we understand only enough to grasp at it, we recognize that this pattern represents, or signifies, means, an apple or an orange, a smile or a frown. We have had to learn to interpret these patterns, just as one would have to learn the Morse code before one could decipher a message sent in its dots and dashes. The ease and sureness with which we recognize commonplace things shows how skilfully we have learned to interpret their images, and also allows us to overlook the part which interpretation plays. We are as unconscious of the series of translations which go on between receiving the visual pattern on the retina and acting on the information we get from it as we are of the complicated chemical changes and interactions by which food received into the stomach is made available for building flesh or providing energy . . .

We see, then, that perception necessarily involves interpretation, even the perception of 'real' things. We are familiar with the idea that certain sorts of perception involve interpretation – the pictures we see in the fire, or in clouds, or in cracks in the ceiling, or the bogies that children see in their twilit bedroom. We recognize that such interpretations vary with the perceiver, and may change with his mood, and we tend to think of visual patterns which stimulate fantasy as sharply distinct from the images of 'real' things like chairs and tables. It is, however, more useful to consider them as lying at the two opposite ends of a continuum. We have learned to interpret images at the 'real' end of the continuum in such a way that we can rely on the information we get from them and use it as a basis for action – we can sit on the chairs we see, and lean on the tables. When such things are illustrated by a photograph or drawing in such a way that the retinal image sufficiently resembles the retinal image of the 'real' thing, we interpret it in the same way as the image of the thing itself. For all practical purposes, most of us interpret these images in the same way, we agree about what we see, the range of variation in the information the pattern gives to different people is narrow. At the other, 'fantasy', end of the continuum we can place images which different people interpret in all sorts of different ways. These also may be the images of 'real' things like clouds, or pictures of them, but the perceiver 'sees' them as something quite different. At this end we can place the inkblots used in the Rorschach test to which individuals react so variously that they can be used as a test of personality. The information obtained from images at the 'fantasy' end of the continuum is not checked by acting on it.

Near the inkblots we could place 'abstract' works of art over which people notoriously differ. Next would come more representational pictures, such as those of human situations used for another kind of personality test (the Murray Thematic Apperception Test) which are differently interpreted by different people. Some works of art which are partly ambiguous, for instance the smile on the face of Leonardo's *Mona Lisa*, would come here. Still nearer to the 'real' end we could place more realistic paintings which give rise to little variation in interpretation among observers with roughly the same background of experience.

An interesting experiment has shown, however, that what is seen in even representational pictures may be affected by extraneous conditions. The experiment was done using Breughel's *Peasant Wedding*. The subjects were told a story about two families that had quarrelled for generations . . . The wedding feast was described, taking place in conditions of restlessness and suppressed excitement. A few days later the subjects were asked to choose from seven pictures the one which was most relevant to the story, and they all chose the *Peasant Wedding* . . . When the subjects were asked to recall the picture after a few days or weeks it was clear that their recollections of it were strongly affected by the story. They mentioned details in the picture which had played an important part in the story, such as the sheaves of corn on the wall, but ignored others that were equally prominent to the control subjects who had not heard the story. They also gave these details meanings which were quite different than those given to the picture by the control subjects. The bridegroom, for instance, was described as 'sad and downcast', the musicians as men carrying ash-staves, and the crowd at the back of the room as unruly. Subjects who were asked to retell the story showed the same kind of effect of selection and distortion. The information obtained from one experience had become associated with, and modified by, that obtained from the other.

In everyday life or in specific learning situations, pieces of information which may or may not have useful relevance to each other become associated and affect each other's meaning . . . We try to transmit the same information to all observers, to work at the 'real' end of the continuum rather than at the 'fantasy' end. However, it is worth noting that a certain image could be at one end of the continuum for some kinds of people and at the opposite end for others. Radiographs for radiologists would be near the real end, for however sharply they disagree over their interpretations, they differ only within a limited range and they can check the information they get from pictures by other tests. But for people who do not understand them, radiographs can evoke as wide a range of interpretations as inkblots, and as they cannot check their interpretations they remain fantastical.

The Influence of Individual Assumptions upon Perception

From M.L. Johnson, 'Theory of free group discussion', *Health Education Journal*, 11, 3, 112–17, 1953.

Teaching and learning would be easy if the jug and bottle notion of education were a valid one. According to this way of looking at the relationship of teacher and taught, the learner is an empty vessel ready to be filled. If he is anxious to learn, we can assume that the bottle is uncorked and the only difficulty there seems to be in the way of his receiving the contents of the jug is the narrowness of his neck. However, if the jug pours skilfully enough, some at least of its contents will get into the bottle and it is taken for granted that after the transfer the bottle will contain the same *kind* of substance, if not the same amount as left the jug. This, however, is far from true of learning. A more useful analogy is with an organism in relation to its food. The learner is more like a biological system separated from the things he needs to absorb by *selectively* permeable membranes. Not all of the materials presented in the food can get across the wall of the gut, but only certain of them, and most of these have to undergo change before they can be taken in – they have to be digested. Which parts are absorbed and which rejected depends not only on the nature of the meal, but on the digestive equipment of the organism, and many other conditions. Two people, or even the same person at different times, eating the same food will absorb different products of digestion in different amounts according to many interacting factors (for instance, the bacterial flora of the gut, the state of the muscles of the gut wall, and the biochemical constituents of the blood). Nor have we finished with change when the foods have got across the gut wall and entered the blood stream. They will be differently modified in the processes of assimilation by the cells, as molecules are broken down and their parts reassorted.

In an analogous fashion, learners are selective and transformative: the information which gets across and is used is never quite the same as was given. However carefully we choose our words, even in ordinary conversation, the information received may be very different from what we intended. The recipient's reaction to our communication may therefore be unexpected . . .

When the learner is being taught by straightforward didactic methods as in a lecture (and this also applies to visual aids) there is no 'feed-back' to the teacher; he cannot know what is selected or how what is absorbed is distorted. He can only try to present the material in a manner which, from his judgement of the listeners' backgrounds, he considers interesting and unambiguous, so that they will absorb as much, and in as undistorted a form, as possible. The more heterogeneous the audience and the more unfamiliar the lecturer is with it, the more likely it is that there will be serious distortion in the information accepted, the more difficult it is for the lecturer to guess correctly to what extent this is happening. 'Any questions?' after a lecture is meant to offer opportunity to put this right, but has limited value. The more confused the listener is, the more need he has to ask questions, the more difficult it is to frame useful ones, the more difficult it is for the lecturer to answer in a helpful way. The greatest difficulty is that the listener usually does not know how much he has missed, how much misunderstood, and so cannot ask questions where they are most necessary.

At this point you may object that I seem to talk about the transmitting of information only, rather than the modifying of attitudes. Perhaps it is not really useful to separate the two in thinking about education. Attitudes are certainly modified by information, more or less, according to how the information is assimilated. But attitudes determine what information is taken in and how it is used. Information and attitudes are continually interacting.

Let us examine a little more closely what determines the processes of selection and modification of information. We recognize that the factors which influence a person's reaction to a piece of information are many and varied, and that some of these are more or less under our control – we choose the time and place to make an announcement, we acknowledge that often it is not so much what you say as the way you say it that matters. Certain other factors are less under our immediate control – those we roughly call the attitude of the recipient. Each person has a multitude of interacting assumptions about the nature of the world into which the new information must somehow be integrated. These assumptions have themselves been made as a result of receiving information from the environment in the past; together they form our 'assumptive world'. Each person develops his own unique assumptive world – the world as it seems to him. As Cantril *et al.* (1949) put it:

The world man creates for himself through what Einstein has called 'the rabble of the senses' is one that takes on a degree of order, system, and meaning as man builds up through tested experience a pattern of assumptions and expectancies on which he can base action.

This concept of human behaviour has developed largely as a result of research on the way people react to visual stimuli. (It is worth noting that we refer to a person's attitudes as his outlook, views or ways of looking at

things.) As a very simple illustration let us take the case of how we see
playing cards. Playing cards are usually of a standard size and shape. From
the information supplied to us by any one playing card, we learn to make
assumptions as to its size and shape, and as to the size and shape of all
playing cards. The 'stimulus pattern' of a playing card (the image which
falls on the retina, which may be imitated by suitable optical arrangements
of lenses and screen to represent the eye) varies according to its position
relative to the eye. The size of the image will vary with distance, and its
shape will be much more often trapezoidal than rectangular. When we are
playing a game of cards, the sizes and shapes of the stimulus patterns of
the cards are continually changing; even if the cards are lying still the stimulus pattern changes with every flick of our eye. But we learn to interpret
these differing stimulus patterns and assume a certain size and shape for
the playing cards. Every time we put out our hand to pick up a card, we are
both using our assumptions as to its size and shape to determine its position,
and *testing* them. If we play with standard cards long enough we learn to
make verifiable assumptions on which we can base effective action. In ordinary circumstances such assumptions are useful. But if we are presented
with non-standard cards, we may go on using the assumptions we learned
to make for standard cards and be led astray. For instance, if a person is
shown playing cards of different sizes placed at the same distance in an
otherwise dark room, he assumes them to be of the same standard size, but
at different distances, the smaller one further away, the larger one nearer.
As long as he does not attempt to act on the assumptions, he keeps them,
but if he tries to touch the large card he will not stretch far enough, and
if he tries to touch the smaller one he will stretch too far. His assumptions
are not useful in these conditions, and if he is to act effectively he must
modify them. If his *assumptions are not modifiable he is unable to take in the new
piece of information* – that playing cards of non-standard size exist; he cannot
see such cards as the size they 'really' are, nor at their correct distance.
Again, people shown momentarily a *red* six of clubs have great difficulty in
seeing it as such. They tend to report black clubs, or red hearts, or purple
or brown clubs or hearts – what they see is distorted in shape or colour by
their assumptions based on their previous experience of black clubs. If
anomalous cards are seen often enough in suitable circumstances the assumptions as to the nature of cards will change.

It is easy to see how in dealing with things like playing cards we soon
arrive at assumptions which are verifiable, and can be relied upon as guides
to action. As social beings, however, a great deal of our behaviour is concerned with interaction with other people, whose behaviour is much more
complicated and variable than that of physical objects and less amenable to
repeated testing. Assumptions made early in life as to the nature of parents
and other people and one's relations to them profoundly affect later behaviour, and if they are not suitably modified by experience (that is, if new
information is not taken in), they may make satisfactory relationships with
other people difficult to establish.

Each person's 'assumptive world' consists of a mass of assumptions of all kinds concerning, for instance, the size and shape of playing cards, the causation and purpose of illness, the nature of authority, the status of women, the kind of food it is proper to eat, optimism, pessimism and the trust to be placed in human nature . . .

The Effect of Unconscious Learning upon Perception

From 'Changing higher education by the application of some group-analytic ideas'. Paper given at the Eighth International Conference of Group Psychotherapy, Mexico City, April 1984.

... The human brain has been described as the best and cheapest general computer, assembled by unskilled labour. I believe it is mostly used by unskilled labour, and that most of us could improve the usefulness of our own brain by understanding a little better how it works. The trouble is that our conscious behaviour is in part controlled by unconscious processes. Only when we can recognize these can we control them more wisely.

Some examples of unconscious learning which profoundly affect subsequent uptake of information will be given.

Rotating trapezoid

What most people see when they look at this apparatus is a window swinging continually from right to left and back, oscillating as though on a hinge. When a wooden rod is hung on the frame, very strange things happen. One sees the rod move independently of the frame; at one moment it is at right angles to the frame, at another parallel with it, and pressing so hard against it that it suddenly breaks through and appears on the other side. When a small red cube is attached to an upper corner of the window it also appears to have movement independent of the frame. One may see it slide up and down the top edge of the window, or circle the frame like a satellite.

A trapezoid is a four-sided figure with two parallel sides, one shorter than the other. This apparatus consists of a trapezoidal piece of cardboard which is painted to look like a rectangular window seen in perspective. It is mounted on a rotating spindle fixed to the middle of its bottom edge. If we change our position relative to the trapezoid, by tilting it for instance, we can immediately see that it is rotating, not oscillating, swinging backwards and forwards. The explanation of the error of observation is that we are, from the cradle, bombarded with the images of rectangles – common in industrialized buildings and most artefacts – but most of the images thrown onto the retina at the back of the eye will be trapezoidal not rectangular, because the objects are seen in perspective. So we equate trapezoidal images on our retinas, inside ourselves, with rectangles in the real world outside. Of course, actual trapezoids also throw trapezoidal images, but trapezoids are rare, especially among windows. As the trapezoid rotates its shorter side comes to the front, but we do not see it at the front, because this would conflict with our assumption that what is outside us is a rectangle – so we see the short side always at the back, further away, and the long side always at the front. Consequently, the window seems to swing as though on a hinge and not to rotate on the spindle at its middle. We cannot see the trapezoid as it really is, nor the rod or the cube when we see them in relation to it, because of our assumption that it is a rectangle. People from cultures who do not live in a rectangle-dominated world do not experience the illusion as we do.

I want to emphasize, first, that we are quite unaware of the assumption that we are using, and therefore cannot evaluate its effect on our perception, on our understanding of what we are looking at; second, that we see the thing differently if we change our position relative to it; and third, that we modify the 'truth' by trying to make sense of the new thing – to fit it in to our past experience of relevant things.

Photograph of the boiler of a battleship

You see the small bosses, convex rivets which hold the metal plates together, and the large irregular concave dents, made by shell fire. Turn the photograph upside down, and the rivets become dents and the dents blisters. In normal life the light comes constantly from above, whether from sun or moon or stars, or artificial light. We learn to interpret shapes with a shadow at the top as dents, as concave, and those with a shadow below as bumps, as convex. What we perceive depends on our relationship with the thing we are looking at.

Photograph of a tin of tomatoes, a tin of beef, and a tin of baby food

This is another example of our tendency to expect constancy of frequently experienced events. Some doctors working with a primitive tribe, educating the people about diet, were asked: 'But why do white men eat babies?' White men were seen to eat a lot of food out of tins with labels illustrating the contents such as tomatoes, beef (a cow's head) and . . . a bonny baby's smiling face on a tin containing puree of apricots and rice.

This propensity to store experiences which occur frequently in such a way that they unconsciously influence present experiences can help us to interpret and react swiftly to a recurrence of the same or similar events. But they may lead us astray in rapidly changing conditions, where they may be used inappropriately, and help us to be resistant to seeing change. Our minds are stuffed full with general ideas, attitudes, or expectations – which we have collected unintentionally, are unaware of, and therefore do not evaluate.

Early Experiences and Intellectual Habits

From 'Summing up', in Sandler, M. and MacKeith, R. (eds)
Psychosomatic Aspects of Paediatrics, Report of Practical Study Group
of Royal College of Physicians, 146–8, 1961.

I hope nobody supposes I shall be objective (in my summing up) just
because I am not a paediatrician, psychiatrist, or general practitioner. And,
in spite of what Dr Wisdom said about my interest in teaching, I shall not
try to tell you what you have learnt. I shall try to give you my worm's-eye
view, reminding you that what seemed a diamond to me may be just a grain
of sand to you . . .

Among the most intransigent of the difficulties that arose (in the conference) was our common tendency to think dichotomously. Why is it so
much easier to think in terms of 'either/or' than of 'both/and'? Dr Miller
said that the highest intellectual functions have a visceral and somatic history, and I would suggest that this particular intellectual habit may be something to do with our having had only one mother. It is true, of course, that
the child had two breasts to suck, but it can suck at only one at a time, and
has to be physically displaced, turned round from right to left, with goodness knows what insult to its spatial orientation, if it is to be offered one
teat instead of the other. As a biologist I like to consider possible optima
and not norms only. The feeding arrangements for piglets are probably
less conducive to the formation of dichotomous thinking habits, because
they can more easily range up and down a series of equally nice alternative sources of supply than our babies can. This may explain the notable absence of the dichotomous thinking syndrome in pigs, though I would not
have learnt much from this conference if I went away thinking it was likely
to be the only cause . . .

Authority-Dependency as an Obstacle to Learning

From 'Changing higher education by the application of some group-analytic ideas'. Paper given at the Eighth International Conference of Group Psychotherapy, Mexico City, April 1984.

... I think the authority-dependency relationship is at the centre of our difficulties with learning.

Reproduction of woodcut: Medieval classroom

The set-up for teaching factual knowledge is indicated in the picture of a medieval school room, which is a caricature of the set-up in many modern school rooms or lecture halls. The authority of the teacher is exaggerated by several features which are extraneous to his scholarship. He sits on a higher seat than the pupils, wears a high hat, has a bigger book propped up on a lectern which also serves to separate him from the children, has a birch to beat them if they are naughty and an assistant to ridicule them with a donkey's head if they are stupid. It is an asymmetric relationship – the teacher talks, the children listen and occasionally speak to him (usually only if spoken to) but are not supposed to speak or listen to each other. If they have learnt the lesson, they can reproduce what the teacher said to his satisfaction. They have no other ways of knowing right from wrong. The acquisition of knowledge becomes intimately associated with the students' relationship to the teacher, and to other authority figures.

We learn from adults in other ways, for instance by imitating them, and so by paying close attention to their behaviour.

Photograph of young child pushing wheelbarrow

In a photograph of a child pushing a full-sized wheelbarrow we see him imitating a grown-up and supporting himself with a grown-up's tool – he can hardly walk on his own.

Photograph of boy watching father

A two-and-a-half-year-old, watching his father mend a toy, has every muscle tense. Would that students paid such fascinated attention to what we would like to teach them!

Picasso, *Young Acrobat on Ball*

In Picasso's *Young Acrobat on Ball* the youth is practising in the presence of his father, a monumental seated figure, seemingly not actually watching his son, but massively there.

These are surely better figures for children to imitate than the dogmatic medieval teacher. Rembrandt's sketch of two old women with a child learning to walk is much better than the medieval school woodcut as a model of what education should be. The child wears a padded hat in case he falls; the women do not teach him, so much as encourage and support him – note that they bend over towards him, unlike the medieval teacher increasing his height. They help him into a future of a condition unfamiliar to them, beyond their imagination.

Teachers who adopt group analytic principles could be more like Rembrandt's old women than the medieval teacher, providing the student with a crash helmet and pointing to the future, his, that they will never see. Or even like a wheelbarrow, a grown-up's artefact that a toddler can lean on and learn how to manoeuvre. Or like the grown-up with Picasso's young acrobat, watching the boy learning, a massive, silent figure, but a comforting one. One has to be in authority, in order to be able to share it with the group. One does not aim to establish anti-authoritarian attitudes, but rather to encourage each student to become an authority in his own right.

Professional Education for an Unknown Future

From 'The nature and nurture of architects', *Transactions of the Bartlett Society*, 2, 53–82, 1965.

... There seem to be two main tasks in training for the professions: the task of passing on to the student an increasingly large and complex body of knowledge which it is necessary for him to master before he can practise his profession, and that of preparing him to continue to learn, to adapt his skills to changing conditions, and even initiate change himself, to be inventive or creative.

It is probably true to say that university education is better adapted to deal with the first than with the second. The second task, of training people for change, is less tangible. There are not well-attested techniques for predicting how adaptable or original a candidate will be as a student, much less as a practitioner during thirty or forty years of professional life. Deliberate attempts made during the course to encourage adaptability do not go much beyond exposing the student to intellectual change, making him aware of the history of the subject or setting him a good example by doing research in it. Yet important though the first task is, the second is becoming increasingly so. In conditions of rapid technological change, the body of knowledge and specific skills quickly gets out of date; we must prepare our students for an unknown future.

Innovation, Creativity and Training

From *Innovation and Training* (source and date unknown).

My title may seem to express a coupling of opposites: innovation is the introduction of novelty, the alteration of something established; to be trained is to be taught how to do something already known, to be drilled to follow prescribed rules. To innovate is to create, to burst out of the rut; to be trained is to learn how to stay within it. Innovation carries overtones of glamour, of daring, and is admired, while training is worthy of approval as being somewhat dull, boring, repetitive. Innovation seems to come by grace, and training by industry. There is a tendency to think that innovators, inventors or creators are born rather than made, and indeed that training is likely to spoil them, however good and necessary it may be for those less well endowed. So the title calls to mind several opposites: old and new; conforming and nonconforming; structure and freedom; work and play. I shall attempt to show, mostly with visual illustrations [omitted throughout], how important the interaction of these opposites is for the processes of innovation.

I do not think people are so naive about this seeming antithesis between training and inventiveness in engineering (and science generally) as they are about it in the arts. Nobody is so silly to think that bridges can be made to stand up, or tunnels to burrow, or aeroplanes to fly, by untrained engineers. But there is an echo of the same way of thinking perhaps in the tendency, in university education, to separate in time and place the laying of the foundations of theory and the applying of them in design; or in science, making students learn about the old for three long undergraduate years and suddenly permitting them to try to find out something new, to do research, for a second degree . . .

The old and the new

The problem for educators is how to transmit to the pupil the essential body of knowledge and skills in such a way that he can use them not only repetitively, parrot-fashion when that is required, for it often is, but also in a flexible, inventive way, as the basis for innovation when that is desirable. Harlow's experiments with young monkeys confronted with a strange situation will illustrate the importance of a secure base from which to explore and manipulate. Structure is necessary for freedom. The teacher must impart self-confidence as well as knowledge.

The psychological processes of taking in information new to oneself and of thinking up something new are not all that different. Both are concerned with the making, breaking and remaking of patterns . . . New information can be taken in only at the cost of restructuring the assumptions or expectations, based on previous experience of similar things, which one automatically and unconsciously uses in interpreting a stimulus pattern.

But however difficult it is to break with the old, new things cannot come out of nothingness, but only out of old things. Nothing as elaborately organized as Botticelli's Venus, with or without her wisp of veil, ever came out of an empty sea. For the creation of life the most that could be expected would be a few atoms linked to form complex molecules. Even in the arts, the early products of great innovators show strongly how much they have inherited from their predecessors. Some early pictures of Picasso look quite conventional, and one might be forgiven for assigning some of Beethoven's early works to Mozart. And at a practical level, long after our ancestors had learned how to make pots without needing to shape them in a mould of basketwork, they marked them with the ghosts of baskets; and similarly, the first motor cars mimicked horse carts.

So innovators need to learn a lot, and one of the outstanding characteristics of creative people is their prodigious industry. Even if the flash of inspiration comes effortlessly as though a gift, it only comes to the prepared mind, and after hard preparatory work. Creative people are intensely perceptive and receptive; painters look a lot, musicians listen a lot. Creative writers read a lot: 'I've read almost everything', Coleridge said; and his faery world of the *Ancient Mariner* was built on lore as substantial as that achieved by chasing up, with patience and passion, references in the *Proceedings of the Royal Society*, just like any well-trained scientist. Like Darwin, he filled enough notebooks with comments on his reading to keep PhD students busy for years to come.

A lot of biographical evidence has been gathered about the work-style of creative people – scientists, painters, writers. From this, it seems that the psychological processes involved consist of a combination of conscious and 'unconscious', or rather 'preconscious' processes – of intense, directed, willed work, and of flashes of inspiration or insight, which come apparently spontaneously, dropping into the mind unbidden, unexpected. But in the classic case of Poincaré, mathematician, physicist, philosopher, whose autobiographical accounts we are fortunate to have, the will-controlled work, and the unwilled inspiration seem, sometimes at least, to have occurred at different times, and indeed in different places, at relaxed, off-guard moments, or when the conscious mind was concerned with other things. He described his work on the theorem of Fuchsian functions as follows:

Naturally, I proposed to form all these functions. I laid siege to them systematically and captured all the outworks one after the other. There was one, however, which still held out, whose fall would carry with it that of the central fortress. But all my efforts were of no avail at first, except to make me better understand the difficulty, which was already something. All this work was perfectly conscious.

He continues:

Thereupon, I left for Mont-Valerien, where I had to serve my time in the army, and so my mind was preoccupied with very different matters. One day as I was crossing the street, the solution of the difficulty which had brought me to a standstill came to me all at once ...

This passage illustrates the deep personal involvement, the sense of struggle but also of fun that accompanies some innovative achievements.

Needless to say, when the research worker comes to write up his observations, experiments, hypotheses and ideas, the temporal pattern he presents has little similarity to the way the work actually progressed. Indeed, the actual pattern would not only be for many workers difficult to reconstruct, but for most readers it would be very difficult to understand. The formulation has to be made in conventional mode before it is comprehensible. This may be one reason why the inspirational components of scientific work tend to be overlooked, and the basic similarities of the creative process in arts and sciences are therefore minimized. This difference between presentation and process makes one doubt the universal applicability of any highly systematic, logical or rational recipe for design.

Breaking patterns

The knowledge absorbed does not, of course, remain an undigested lump. The ability to break up wholes, to use their parts in different combinations, is an important feature of the creative act. In some cases the inspiration seems to be born out of the worker's continued efforts to arrange and rearrange the elements, maybe laboriously, maybe playfully, trying this way and that to find the most satisfying pattern by manipulating paint, or stone, or words, or facts, as the case may be. Here again, there is no sharp boundary between copying, that is, conforming, and inventing ...

Creating by destroying

Innovation demands a coming to terms with destruction; by definition, the more brilliant the invention, the newer it is, the deeper and more widespread are the changes in the old that it demands. This is obviously true of new ways of thinking. To accept that the world is round when you had thought it flat, that man has risen from the brutes not fallen from the angels as you had been brought up to believe, or that babies' heads are full of quite nasty as well as quite nice things when you had supposed them to be as pure as they are empty, to accept such ideas at the times when they were revolutionary, must have involved a wholesale modification of vast complexes of associated ideas, attitudes and habits of thinking.

Note that it is not only with the destruction of other people's ideas but also of his own that the inventor has to come to terms, that simply in order to have a new idea, he has to modify, even to destruction, those general attitudes and ways of thought that he has inherited. Further, the inventor has had to destroy one after another of his own creations in the exhaustive search for the best one. Darwin said:

> I have steadily endeavoured to keep my mind free so as to give up any hypothesis, however much beloved (and I cannot resist forming one on every subject) as soon as facts are seen to be opposed to it. Indeed, I have had no choice but to act in this manner, for with the exception of the Coral Reefs I cannot remember a single first-formed hypothesis which had not after a time to be given up or greatly modified.

Perhaps 'destroy' is too harsh a word, because some workers talk of playing or toying with ideas, but Picasso speaks forthrightly of destroying: 'With me a picture is a sum of destruction; I make a picture and proceed to destroy it' (but he goes on to say that in the end nothing is lost).

So to produce creatively, it is necessary not only to transcend the old, but to accept responsibility for its dissolution.

Born or made?

Undoubtedly creativity, like all things good and bad, tends to run in families, but creative people have not only been born into creative families, they have also been brought up in them, and the way they are brought up, both at home and at school, and the conditions in which they work when they are grown up, are important. A social environment that provides rich and varied experiences, encourages curiosity, permits puzzlement, gives a sense of security without demanding rigid conformism, fosters independence and self-reliance, and sets an example of purposeful enjoyable work, will help to encourage creativity in people, whether or not they have inherited a terrific intellectual endowment.

An important feature of the social environment is the authority-dependency relationship (the old and new again). Caws (1969), asking why discovery is inhibited in all but a few of the much larger number capable of it, cites biographical evidence (for example, of Darwin and Freud) that many men of genius have been

> characterized by a strong resistance to authority (that is, resistance to having their conclusions drawn for them) and, at the same time, by an openness to random suggestion amounting almost to credulity . . .

Ordinary social experience, and especially education, works, of course, in precisely the opposite sense, imposing, even in the most well-meaning of democracies, an extraordinarily authoritarian view of the world and, at the same time, encouraging the belief that a man should be selective about what he takes in, and sceptical about all evidence from non-authoritarian sources. These tendencies alone would be enough to account for the inhibition of discoveries in all but a handful of the population at any given time.

I cannot resist putting in a plug for my own panacea for this, and indeed for most of society's deficiencies – the value of gaining better understanding about human interaction. Granted the creative urge has an essentially personal, individualistic component, the difficulty is that many of the problems of today cannot be solved by individuals. There is great resistance to the notion of group work as being creative; the need to excel personally conflicts with the need to collaborate. As we have seen, innovators have always depended on past achievements ('If I have seen further than others,' said Newton, 'it is because I have stood on the shoulders of giants'.) Taking from the pool of ideas of the dead, contributing to the pool of ideas available to the unborn, these can be done, though difficult enough. But what for many of us is insuperable, is contemporaneous collaboration. Why should this be so, and must it continue to be so?

Emotional Security as a Condition for Change

From M.L. Johnson, 'Theory of free group discussion', *Health Education Journal*, 11, 3, 112–17, 1953.

... For the educationist a significant thing about assumptive worlds is that they are built up largely in an unconscious, non-rational, non-intellectual way. Most of us, most of the time, are no more conscious of most of our assumptions than we are of the movement of the Earth – we are one with them, as with it. We can, however, undertake to find out that the Earth moves by comparing it with other heavenly bodies. Similarly, we can study our own assumptive world by comparing it with somebody else's, for no two people have exactly the same assumptive world. When we have become aware of what assumptions we are making we are in a better position to change them if they do not lead to effective action. It is the aim of free group discussions to make this possible.

... A permissive atmosphere is essential because people must not be allowed to feel afraid of making fools of themselves by exposing the irrationality of their thinking and feeling. They must feel free to talk in a spontaneous, even incoherent and random manner, so that assumptions can be brought to light and their usefulness examined. It will be found that many of them, though relevant for the particular person, are strictly speaking irrelevant to the main issue ... Let us see how this works out if we are, for instance, trying to persuade a mother to adopt 'demand' feeding. The new piece of information we want her to accept and use is that demand feeding is better for the child than three- or four-hourly feeding. There may be no difficulty at all in getting her to accept this – her assumptions about babies may be ... that they are just like animals, and who heard of a cat watching the clock? On the other hand she may resent any suggestion of the animal nature of motherhood; she may think that a good mother controls the child; a good mother does not allow the child to control her, because it would soon become uncontrollable; she does not give the baby what it wants whenever it wants it, because it must learn to tolerate disappointment and so on ... The information may be very disquieting – for instance, a mother who has already fed a child three-hourly may feel herself criticized, and she may be anxious about the harm she may have done to the child; if she herself had been brought up on the old system, she may even worry about her own mental health. It may therefore be easier to reject the information – to believe that demand feeding is *not* better. Whether or not she is able to accept and act on the new information depends on the extent to which all these interacting assumptions can be modified. The aim of free group discussions is to establish conditions in which she can become consciously aware of her assumptions in a situation in which it is possible to examine them and modify them.

This brings us to another reason why the permissive atmosphere is essential. The more important the new information is and the more changes its assimilation demands, the more difficult it is to accept it, the greater is the incentive to refuse to act on it, and instead to go on in the old way. Change itself is bound to be associated with anxiety, and matters of health are for most people surrounded by it . . . In the permissive atmosphere of free group discussions anxiety can be expressed and then allayed by the supporting action of the group; conditions are established in which the reorganizing of assumptive worlds is facilitated . . .

There is nothing very new in this; travel (that is, meeting people with different assumptive worlds) has long been known to broaden the mind, and 'talking it over' (in a permissive atmosphere) to help one to clear one's ideas, and to make up one's mind to a course of action. In free group discussion we attempt to direct more consciously and intensively the learning processes which occur in ordinary life.

Emotional Aspects of Learning in Professional Education

From M.L. Johnson, 'Human relations and the medical student', *Medical World*, July, 1–4, 1958.

A student learns far more from his teachers than what is prescribed in the curriculum, as well as far less. The body of knowledge in which a medical student must be instructed is fairly clearly laid down. The extent to which he has absorbed this body of knowledge, and the effectiveness with which in certain specified circumstances he can use it, is tested by examination. In this way, if not during the actual process of teaching, the teacher becomes aware that what the student shows he has learnt differs both in quantity and kind from what the teacher thought he was teaching him. The body of knowledge has shrunk a little in transmission, and of the facts that have not got lost, some have become distorted. There has been, if not a failure of communication, at least an inefficiency. As for the student, it is the tendency to shrinkage rather than distortion that impresses and depresses him; gaps in knowledge are easily spotted; it is much more difficult to detect one's own misunderstandings.

This selective aspect of learning has not, of course, escaped the notice of the many bodies that have deliberated on medical education . . . And as a result of the work of such bodies the curriculum has in fact been periodically subject to major revisions, expansions and reductions, as well as to continual small and local modifications made by the teachers themselves in daily practice.

Sensory data

I stress that it is the *curriculum* that has been evaluated and reformed in this way – though still leaving much to be desired in the graduate it produces – because I want to return to my first point, that the student learns far *more* than what is prescribed and testable in examinations. I refer to the mass of information he picks up as it were through the pores of his skin, without design or effort, from the cultural milieu of the medical school. Only parts of the information displayed before the student in this way have been deliberately designed by the teaching body with the same conscious discrimination as has the structure of the curriculum. Much of it, many basic unquestioned assumptions and attitudes, the teachers express inadvertently through their personalities, modulated in a variety of ways and to differing extents by the tradition of the school and its present inhabitants. What impinges on the student is a welter of sensory data representing this microcosm – the result of the behaviour of innumerable people in sensitive interaction with the physical and organic environment. Taken in by the student as unwittingly as they are displayed, these impressions, assumptions or attitudes are not amenable to critical evaluation. But they are subject to selection and distortion by the receiver; they are no more taken in whole and unchanged than is the curriculum.

Nature of response

It is to this background to the curriculum, to the social situation in which learning takes place, that I want to draw attention. To sharpen the issue, we may draw on a considerable volume of information which shows the importance for learning of generalized sensory experience to which there may be, apparently, no immediate directed or purposeful response. Puppies or rats treated as household pets are more mature in their behaviour than are siblings reared in cages; children brought up by fosterparents as members of a family have higher intelligence quotients than those reared in institutions; stimuli that are innocuous if given to young goats when the mother is present may establish an experimental neurosis if the young are alone. To use Hebb's useful formulation, any sensory event may be considered as having potentially two functions: it may elicit a specific response ('cue function') and it may help to tune up the nervous system and predispose it to react in certain ways to cues ('arousal function'). In the medical course intentional teaching – lectures, demonstrations, ward rounds – may be regarded as having mainly a 'cue function'. The general background of stimulation from the medical school environment, on the other hand, has mainly an 'arousal function': it affects the learning process in ways that are little controlled and not fully appreciated . . .

Some features of the social and psychological situation of the medical student thrust him back into an emotionally insecure state, in which 'the neglect of the critical study of principles and of independent thought' can grow.

Student as trainee

Compared with other members of their age group, medical students are in an anomalous position. In common with other professional trainees the responsibilities of adulthood are delayed for most of them; they remain financially dependent at an age when they could be earning their own living, marrying and bringing up children. At the same time they are preparing to undertake responsibilities of a peculiarly heavy and demanding kind, of intimate involvement with other people's lives, with birth, suffering and death.

Personality factors

It may be that in the first years the preclinical sciences act as an antiseptic or detoxicating buffer between the schoolroom and the ward, but I doubt whether the transition is either as painless or as fruitful as it could be. The implications of the dissecting room, for instance, are many and complex; by dissecting the dogfish, frog or rabbit the student is little prepared for the emotional impact of what is probably his first intimate dealings with a human corpse. That this experience has been too much for some people, Charles Darwin for example, one can hardly regret. What is more important is the part this sensory input plays in the learning of the student who continues with medicine. At what cost in increasing the difficulties of learning anatomy, in stultifying scientific curiosity, or in loss of general sensitivity, does the student come to terms with an activity which to ordinary people is loaded with fear, horror and disgust?

I am not suggesting a cotton-wool alternative. Medicine is an exacting profession, and no good is served by pretending otherwise, certainly not to the prospective recruit. What I am suggesting is that it may be profitable to consider the medical student not merely as an empty vessel waiting to be filled with the curriculum, but as a person much as other people are, bringing to his learning an interacting complex of likes and dislikes, hopes and fears, prejudices and skills, with which somehow or other his medical studies must become integrated . . .

It is with the processes of adaptation, at present wasteful if not painful, that the student needs help, not only to make him happier, but to make him more efficient . . . I am suggesting that it might be useful to recognize aspects of the student other than his ignorance of the matter of the curriculum, just as doctors are being urged to consider aspects of the patient other than the symptoms they complain of. This approach would itself quicken the students' understanding of the need, and the techniques, for treating the patient-as-a-whole. The ways of behaving to patients that the young doctor adopts are conditioned not only by the rules that have been enunciated and that he has been exhorted to follow, not only by the ways in which he has witnessed his teachers behaving in similar circumstances and that he is invited to imitate, but also by how his elders have treated him when he was in their care, as the patient now is in his . . .

Individual Assumptions as Obstacles to Change

From 'The difficulties of changing', in *Health Care in a Changing Setting: the UK experience.* Ciba Foundation Symposium 43 (new series). Elsevier Excerpta Medica, 319, 1976.

... Some of our assumptions, those concerned more with values and ideas than tangible physical things, are not so easily tested, corrected and refined by feedback. One of these is the commonly held idea that illness is a punishment for wrongdoing. A summary of the results of public opinion surveys on causation of cancer stated that 15–20% of people believed that cancer was connected with immorality. A snatch of conversation between two characters in Solzhenitsyn's *Cancer Ward* (1971) illustrates how one of them ponders on the possible mechanisms of cancer control and in so doing finds a rational basis to support the belief that cancer is related to guilt, while the other, less sophisticated one who needs no such support from science, recognizes his sins and feels that they have doomed him hopelessly:

> 'So I wouldn't be surprised', Kostoglotov continued, 'if in a hundred years' time they discover that our organism excretes some kind of caesium salt when our conscience is clear, but not when it's burdened, and that it depends on this caesium salt whether the cells grow into a tumour or whether the tumour resolves.' Yeffrem sighed hoarsely, 'I've mucked so many women about, left them with children hanging round their necks. They cried . . . mine'll never resolve.'

It is easy to see how such beliefs prevent people from seeking medical aid, or discourage them from taking any steps to prevent cancer; to do so, with their intrapsychic set-up, would be illogical.

Two basic assumptions about the role of the doctor deeply affect his education and are resistant to change because, like primitive beliefs about causation of disease, they are not easily open to test: first, the concept that the doctor is one who *does something* to an inert patient; and second, the idea that his education should be based on the natural sciences. I speak of 'the doctor', but I mean all people concerned with curing the sick.

Crudely, the doctor is seen as a person who makes a sick person well. In pre-scientific days he could do this from a distance, invoking other powers through spells, but more usually nowadays he relies on direct physical intervention, adding things to the body (chemicals) or subtracting bits from it (operating and, not so long ago, bleeding) or, if sufficiently open to oriental culture, sticking pins in and waggling them about. The patient is preferably inert, for an active one is not always active in the right direction; he may accept the gift of a bottle of medicine, but not swallow the correct dose at the right time; lots of bottles are left half empty, as though the drug does as much good magic on the shelf as in the body. In hospital, the extreme of regression is encouraged by taking away the patient's clothes. Listen again to Solzhenitsyn. *Cancer Ward* was staffed with most erudite, highly skilled, utterly devoted doctors. A patient arguing with one of them about his treatment says:

> 'You see, you start from a completely false position. No sooner does a patient come to you than you begin to do all his thinking for him. After that, the thinking's done by your standing orders . . . And once again I become a grain of sand, just like I was in the camp. Once again nothing *depends* on me.'

Related to this concept of the doctor as an all powerful external agent is his initial training in the natural, as distinct from human, sciences. Chemistry, physics and biology, but not sociology or psychology, were and commonly still are prerequisites for entry to medical training, and the study of anatomy, physiology and biochemistry commonly still precedes any contact with patients. Generally, in the premedical and preclinical years the teachers are not medically qualified or, if they are, they have opted out of medical practice. Clinical education is based on the hospital, the patients seen in isolation from their natural physical and social environment. Treatment by the application of technology is emphasized, and the essentially social nature of man is tacitly ignored . . . For instance, the prospectus of a medical school which recently revised its curriculum was lavishly illustrated with about thirty photographs. Most were of impressive buildings and well-equipped laboratories. Two photographs did include patients; in one a patient was being interviewed by a student to get material for the student's research thesis and in the other a patient was prone on a couch, wired up to receive electroconvulsive therapy. Doctors are conditioned for work in hospitals. It is not surprising that, even in the under-developed countries, whose medical ethos is adopted from that of the industrialized West, it is difficult to get doctors to work in community medicine.

The assumption that treatment and prevention of disease must be based on natural science has served us magnificently, facilitating the control of many infectious and deficiency diseases. But it has not got us far enough with diseases that are largely self-induced. It has not stopped people over-eating, or smoking, or worrying, or driving dangerously. The doctor cannot cure such death-dealing habits by putting things into the body or taking things out. It is the difficulties of personal change, of learning and unlearning, that have to be tackled. For each person there is an idiosyncratic tangle of unrecognized and therefore unquestionable assumptions at the root of his disease. Becoming well is a change to which some are resistant . . .

It is not, however, my intention to end on this note of gloom. There are plenty of signs that medical education is moving in the right direction, towards humanizing the curriculum and recognizing the layman as a necessary participant in the treatment and prevention of sickness, his own and other people's. I will make one further point, about the potentialities of discussion groups for facilitating change . . .

Profound or significant changes from the familiar may result in confusion, disorientation, even panic and impotence. Some experiments by Harlow are relevant to our understanding of how to cope with change. Harlow reared baby monkeys on two sorts of substitute mother, both models made of wire, but one was covered with terry-towelling which made it more comfortable to cuddle than the bare wire one. In some experiments the young monkeys had only a wire mother, in others only a terry-cloth mother, but the most interesting cases were the 'dual-reared' ones, that is, those who were suckled on a wire mother, but had a terry-cloth mother, without milk, available to cuddle. The young monkeys reacted differently according to their upbringing and the presence of the mother to frightening situations, such as being confronted with a mechanically moving toy animal or being put in a strange room. Monkeys brought up with a wire mother only, whether she was present or not, appeared to be too terrified by the new experience to take any interest in it, and huddled away in a corner refusing to look. Dual-reared monkeys behaved similarly unless the terry-cloth mother was present; then they would rush to her, and seeming to take comfort and security from contact with her, would turn and look back at the terrifying thing, or be able to explore the strange room. They would cuddle up to her, and make sudden expeditions from this home base to investigate, one after the other, the objects in the room, as a toddler might venture from its mother at a party, returning at intervals for reassurance. A feeling of security was necessary if the monkey was to learn about the strange things. In infancy and childhood, it is the presence of adults that helps us, and, as adults, we commonly look to surrogate parental figures, a doctor perhaps, powerful and caring. But we can learn to get security from peers, in small face-to-face groups, learning to become powerful and caring ourselves. When we have confidence in each other, we can begin to recognize our own assumptions by comparison and contrast with those of others and begin to evaluate their usefulness . . . So groups help us to change by giving us security to perceive differences.

Perception, Communication and Education for Team Work

From 'Integrated building design: the human factor', *Architects Journal*, 581–2, September 1972.

Integrated design implies disparate people bringing disparate elements together to make a new whole. The difficulties of team work are commonly attributed to the different kinds of training that the specialist participants have had, which make it difficult for them to communicate with each other: they 'speak different languages'. They have been inducted into very different subcultures. They now belong to different professional associations or institutes; since leaving school, their education has been different not only in content but also in methods of teaching and examining; it has taken place in buildings that are often geographically separate ... What the participants need to share above all is some understanding of human relationships: this can be acquired at any stage of learning.

The problem is how to make use of each other's experience. Combining in any intellectual endeavour is valuable only to the extent that people's experiences are different. Two similar pairs of hands are better than one in tug of war, or digging a trench, where like is effectively added to like; but when we say 'two heads are better than one', we mean they are better because their contents are different. The skull is thick and impermeable; for the relevant part of its content to be effectively shared, eye-to-eye contact is necessary, the windows of the soul uncurtained, and tongues must wag. It is with some of the factors that affect this interchange of information that I am at present concerned.

I would like to illustrate three simple but basic things about human relationships: the importance of the human face; the importance of proximity and distance between people; and the essentially egocentric nature of each person's view of the world. An understanding of these simple and familiar things may help us to communicate better with each other.

Importance of the human face

The foundations of our fascination with the face are laid early in life. In the human being the arrangements for suckling are such that the baby takes in the nurse's face along with the milk (whereas the last thing a baby goat can see is its nanny-goat's face). The behaviour of the 'nursing couple' ensures that the baby is not only in a position to look at the mother, but actually does so, and babies prefer looking at human face-like diagrams to other figures. Autistic children, who do not learn to communicate, are exceptional in this.

Even in adulthood the face continues to be one of the most interesting and sought-after objects (note the attention paid to it by painters, for instance). It is a powerful source of non-verbal signals; one understands speech very much better if one watches the speaker's face, taking in lip movements and changing expressions and, in particular, movements of the eyeballs. Perception of another's face makes one feel that one understands him better, also that one is better understood by him.

The baby has to work pretty hard to take in the milk, and the muscles of the mouth, tongue and throat are vigorously active while the picture of the mother's face is before his eyes and the sound of her voice in his ears. Coordination of these muscles will later be very important in speech, so that here, in the feeding set-up, the functional necessities for laying the foundations of active communicative behaviour, of reception and expression, are already being built. It is perhaps not surprising that we use feeding metaphors for the taking in of information generally – indigestible facts, regurgitating facts in examination, feeding data to computers, getting feedback.

Proximity and distance

Our earliest communications are through physical contact; while the baby is being fed, his whole body and many senses are stimulated – touch and warmth, smell, taste, sound, vision and movement. The baby's world is multi-sensational and small. Visual and auditory acuity are optimal at close range. A child hears, sees and learns best at mother's knee.

As we grow, the sense of smell deteriorates, we lose sensitivity to high notes, and our eye muscles make it easier to see at greater distances. In middle age we need glasses to bring near objects back into focus. Physical contact remains the most important medium for the expression and acceptance of love. At times of stress, when we naturally regress to a more infantile state, the touch of even a stranger's hand can be enormously comforting. But however skilful we become with the use of words, non-verbal communication continues to be important, sometimes helping us, sometimes hindering us, in conveying accurately what we want to say or in understanding what others want us to understand.

Among these non-verbal factors, spatial relations are very important. Proximity, real or symbolic, continues to matter long after the apron strings have been cut. Lee (1957), in a study of the relation between school journeys and the social and emotional adjustment of young children, found that accessibility to mother was an important factor. It was the child's perception of accessibility that was most important; thus for journeys of approximately equal duration, those involving transport were associated with poorer adjustment than those involving walking only.

Studies of differences between the micro-cultures of hospitals and schools show that behaviour is affected by perception of the accessibility of those in authority. As Revans (1964) has shown, in hospitals the length of stay of patients, which may be taken as indicating their rate of recovery, is related to the wastage rate of nurses, which may be taken as their rate of adjustment to training and work. This in turn is related to how approachable the ward sister regards the doctors and consultants. There are important lessons here.

Sometimes by design, but mostly without the participants being fully aware, spatial arrangements and furniture also play a part in establishing and maintaining various kinds of social interaction. This can be illustrated by the design of schools, lecture theatres and courtrooms, and by behaviour around tables. The round table favoured by King Arthur and his knights remains a powerful symbol of equality of participation. The geographical site of the meeting and the shape of the table were subjects of great concern when arrangements were being made for the Vietnam peace talks.

The egocentric position

Having come together on an even footing, why is communication still so difficult? Communication between people can be efficient only to the extent that they use the same language, and not only use the same words but understand the same thing by them. A great deal of our experiences is highly specific to each individual. We begin by being constitutionally different; from birth we have our own individual fingerprints, and although the surgeons can now give us somebody else's heart, it is very difficult for us to keep it, because of incompatibilities in our biochemistries. And we select, interpret and store information each in our individual way. Each of us occupies the centre of our own world. The egocentric position is so strong in children that they find it very difficult indeed to imagine what it is like to be in somebody else's shoes; so that while at the age of five or six a child can point to his own right hand he will not be able to do this for a person standing opposite him. This requires that he can imagine himself swivelling round through 180 degrees, which is impossible for him at that age.

For messages to pass accurately between two people on personal matters, it is important not only to see things from another's point of view, but especially that one person should be able to see himself as the other person sees him. If the participants are at different levels in the authority-dependency hierarchy this is unusually difficult because of the asymmetry of perception . . .

What to do about it?

Most of this is commonly understood – the difficulties arising from passage and receipt of messages which have been or should already have been formulated. The inefficiencies of communication at all levels in the building industry are only too well known. The people whose individual specialities need to be integrated in production do not get a sufficiently integrated view of the future whole from those who are supposed to have it, the designers and managers. Indeed, so long as the traditional separation of design from construction persists, how can the designers or constructors have an 'integrated' view? To each, 'the whole' is a different 'whole', seen from his egocentric position.

And those who should work together at the bench or at ground level do not communicate among themselves effectively either, because they also have not met face-to-face and talked sufficiently.

There is, however, another source of inefficiency in our present state of human evolution. Not only in production, but more especially at the stage of design and planning, we continue to behave too much as individuals; at present we think of the greatest creative acts as those of single geniuses. It is true that they have used the experience of past generations, could not in fact have produced without it. But there seem to be special barriers between contemporaries which we need to learn how to overcome . . .

I am suggesting that far more concern should be paid to the human factors in communication networks. The expression 'human factor' has negative overtones – we speak of 'human error', 'human failing' or of being 'only human', as something we have to put up with but would prefer to be without. We need to take a more positive view. Abstract messages, however clear and exact, have to be interchanged within the extremely subtle and complex contexts of individuals' minds. It is just as necessary to get some understanding of these contexts as to be able to use 'hardware' skills. It requires time, time spent in face-to-face contact in what may seem to be idle and unproductive ways.

It is easy for a clear-headed, hard-headed person to feel that casual contacts with colleagues, especially those in subordinate positions, are of 'social value' only. He finds many organized discussion meetings frustrating, boring and unproductive; he feels he himself already saw the issues clearly, knew the answers and 'we got nowhere'. What he fails to understand is that we are more likely to get nowhere, or to a nastier place faster, by denigrating the importance of the human factors.

Certainly some instruction and experience to improve understanding of human relationships should be built into technical training (and indeed into general education), but it is never too late to learn and one can never learn enough about it. We need to be more perceptive of the barriers between people, whether equals or of different status. We need to understand the effect of closed office doors, of being kept waiting, of a conversation being interrupted by a telephone call which could have been taken later, of the difference between meeting on neutral ground, or on the territory of the one or the other, of the advantage of playing on home ground. We need to understand that many of these barriers are self-imposed and can be dissolved by changes of attitude – in particular, changes in perception of oneself in relation to other people.

Man is essentially a social animal, but each individual is different from any other. Individuality should not be suppressed but accepted and understood. We have not begun to tap the enormous resources that could be available to the human race if we could only learn better how to share and integrate experience with our contemporaries, not only our forebears, in common endeavour at the highest intellectual levels. We need not only to stand on the shoulders of giants but also to work with them, and with all sizes and shapes of men.

What Does the Institutional Context Communicate to Students?

From 'The work of a university education research unit',
Universities Quarterly, 22, 182–96, 1968.

An educational community

The principle that underlies the work of the unit is similar to that of 'community therapy' which has guided recent work in the treatment of mental illness. In a 'therapeutic community' many features of the institution, administrative, social and personal, are designed to be conducive to helping the patients to learn to behave more effectively. This approach contrasts with the earlier individual approach to the mentally sick, in which each patient was approached as an individual who can be treated apart from the social context, and to whom pills, or electric shock, or psychotherapy were administered, the relationship of the patient as an individual with the doctor, or with members of the ancillary staff, being the only recognized curative factors. Most university teaching is analogous to individual therapy. It is an extension of the infantile learning situation, attention being paid to the absorption of information and skills by an individual in contact with the source of knowledge ... We still have a great deal to learn about the consequences of the interaction of students with each other in various organized group situations, and how to optimize them for different educational purposes. It is imperative that we do learn how to emancipate ourselves from the notion that information comes best from above, to the individual, isolated from the social context. Productive though this situation may be in times of stability, it cannot work effectively in times of rapid change, or produce people who can easily respond to change. There will come a time for each person, when there is no older person left to teach him; he must learn from his agemates, and from those even younger than himself.

If we have not yet sufficiently applied some of the lessons from group dynamics to university education, still less have we applied the lessons of social anthropology, though descriptions of college environments and student characteristics will help us to do this. Ways of behaving are adopted not only from precept, but mostly unconsciously, by passive absorption from the culture, unquestioned and only partly questionable, because only partly verbalized. Usually very little attention is given by authority to the student's perceptions of the culture it establishes. In times of stability there is little need to do so. Teachers will have been subjected to roughly the same educational system as their pupils and can be expected to have roughly the same perceptions of it. But it is otherwise in times of rapid change, when the view that students and staff get of the same events may be very different. It then becomes important to pay careful attention not only to deciding exactly what shall be taught, what body of knowledge and skills shall be transmitted, but what is affecting the students' perceptions besides. Just as a person's understanding of the spoken message depends not only on the words that are said, but also on a multitude of subtle circumstances of the context, of time and place, the sex and age and status of the speaker, his accent and tone of voice, and so on, so what the student learns depends not only on what the teacher intends he shall learn, but on the total impact of the academic experience. It is important therefore to understand how the educational matrix which suffuses the declared substance of the curriculum affects the student, and to ensure that it works in favour of the educational process and not against it. It is also important to ensure that the student gets some understanding of the clues to which he is otherwise unconsciously responding, so that he can get better command over his own behaviour. These are some of the tasks the unit has set itself. It seems appropriate that this should be attempted in a school which is dedicated to improving the education of designers of the built environment, people whose work will profoundly affect the behaviour of thousands of others over long periods of time, in subtle and complex ways they themselves may be quite unaware of.

Social Climate and Freedom to Learn

From 'The nature and nurture of architects', *Transactions of the Bartlett Society*, 2, 53–82, 1965.

... The suggestion that conscious efforts should be made to change people by structuring the social environment, that knowledge of human behaviour should be used to modify it, naturally tends to arouse fears of Big Brother, or in this case the even greater threat of Big Sister. So it is worth emphasizing that these machinations are devised to liberate the individual from arbitrary controls, both external and internal. Granted that always a choice must be made, consciously or unconsciously, from innumerable possible modes of action, then choice should be made in a sophisticated manner, not in ignorance of the alternatives, and not in ignorance of what factors influence each decision (Abercrombie, 1960). The kind of human engineering which, it is argued, may facilitate the development of this understanding must obviously be a corporate undertaking, students and teachers working together. MacKinnon (1962) gives us some advice as to the kind of social climate we should aim at. Discipline, self-control, independence of thought and action, are necessary; new ideas and new possibilities must not be criticized too soon; openness to ideas and experiences must be encouraged; intuitive perception and thinking must be strengthened. In detail, however, it is mostly uncharted territory that we shall be exploring, and it will often be difficult to know who is teaching whom; but the aim is clear, to win greater control for each over his own mental resources. To quote again from Professor Llewelyn-Davies's inaugural address: 'Instead of trying to teach design, we must ... consider how best we can free students from the things that stop them being able to design.'

Part 3

'Associative' Group Discussion in Higher Education

Preface

Part 3 focuses upon 'free', 'analytical' or 'associative' group discussion and the use that has been made of it in higher education. Although this terminology will be unfamiliar to many readers, the issues addressed in this part of the book are ones which daily concern teachers in higher education. Jane Abercrombie examines, for instance, the balance which must be struck between structure and freedom, authority and independence, the affective and cognitive aspects of learning, encouraging students to make and to receive knowledge, the needs of the individual and those of the group, liberal and utilitarian definitions of education. She discusses creativity, assessment and the role and conduct of teachers. She draws attention to the influence of physical settings and institutional cultures, to the pedagogical problems caused by student numbers and to different ways of encouraging peer-supported learning.

At various times she used these adjectives, sometimes in combination, to describe the type of group she used in her own teaching, but she finally decided that 'associative' was the most accurate. She felt that 'free' carried *laissez-faire* overtones which might cause misconceptions, because the essential feature of these groups was not an absence of constraint or structure. Rather, it was that all participants were encouraged to express their personal reactions by associating freely with the topic of discussion and in the process to explore their own unrecognized attitudes, by comparison and contrast with those of others within the group.

It was as a teacher that she first encountered 'associative' group discussion, used in psychotherapy. In *The Anatomy of Judgement* (1969: 17) she claims that it was almost by chance that she became a member of a therapeutic group:

> Realizing that some of these difficulties of 'being scientific' were related to general attitudes or personal predispositions, I had begun to teach through discussion among small groups of students. This

involved . . . a different relationship between teacher and student, and between students, than is usual in university teaching. I soon encountered opposition aroused by the unfamiliarity of the situation, ranging from polite expression of disapproval or bewilderment to scarcely veiled, or even open, hostility. By good chance, I commented to a colleague that this behaviour resembled that of patients in group psychotherapy I had seen reported, and through him I was introduced to a psychiatrist who invited me to see a therapeutic group he was then conducting. This was an illuminating experience for me, and I felt that if one could transfer to a teaching group something of the atmosphere he had established in this therapeutic group, new ways of seeing and thinking might be encouraged. I therefore joined a therapeutic group conducted by Dr S.H. Foulkes, and during some five years of this experience, and of many discussions on group analytic psychotherapy with Dr Foulkes and his associates, I learnt a few simple skills that could be applied to teaching.

Although her own concern was not a therapeutic one, but rather to increase the intellectual and professional potential of her students, she used the vocabulary of group analysis to describe her educational groups. Foulkes (1948: 77), in his 'free associative' groups, encouraged members to 'talk about anything which comes into your head without selection'. He believed that everything that happened within a group, including incidents which took place outside it, but whose influence extended through and into its members, became part of its history, culture and shared experience, that is, of its 'matrix'. So every comment, response, reaction, event which took place in a group had meaning for its members, though everything was open to interpretation at several levels, from the surface to the unconscious, depending on the different needs and abilities of participants. Discussion in the group was therefore 'associative' both because individuals were making their own associations with and around what was happening within the group and in the sense that every contribution was connected with something that had meaning for all members, even if that meaning was discovered only slowly and with the help of the group conductor.

For her part, Jane Abercrombie felt that teaching groups should have more structure than Foulkes believed was necessary in therapeutic groups, even though she encouraged group members to share and enquire into whatever thoughts they had on a subject without keeping to the conventions of rational debate. She usually used some topic to do with members' own work or professional lives as a starting point for discussion. Sometimes the topic was prescribed by the group leader, at others members took it in turns to introduce a subject which was of concern or interest to them. Although the starting point of these learning groups was occupational, she believed that other aspects of the students' lives should have an equal place within the discussion, if the inclusion of them would help individuals towards self-understanding and the modification of their practice. She disclaimed as artificial and sterile teaching methods which maintained a strict distinction between the content that the teacher felt to be important and that which was significant to the learner.

She accepted Foulkes's proposition that it was in a group of people meeting regularly and communicating freely that people could learn about their own unconscious assumptions and attitudes. This learning took place through the comparison of perceptions and the process of what Foulkes called 'corrective interaction' with others. Members could also discover what there was in their present social relationships and the influence of the past upon them that caused them to think and behave as they did. Recognition of these factors could help individuals to gain greater control over their behaviour and begin to change it, if they wished to do so.

She was aware that the education of self and others which went on within an 'associative' discussion group took place only as a result of individual struggle and endeavour. She learnt from Foulkes that group members would often offer strong resistance to one another's interpretations and perspectives, but believed that conflict and the expression of hostile emotions were means towards the improvement of intellectual judgement and professional skill. She therefore stressed the need for a secure environment for learning and showed that associative discussion could take place most easily when the atmosphere of the group was 'permissive'; that is, when it facilitated individual contributions, encouraged risk-taking, enabled communication and the negotiation of mutual understanding and offered support to those engaged in personal change. She drew attention to the painful and frightening effect upon individuals of the questioning by themselves and others of their basic assumptions, of accepting the socio-historical reasons for these and changing their behaviour in the light of their new learning:

> The course brought the student face to face with the need for continual change in himself, if he is to take in more of the information available to him. In some circumstances, such a message could be so painful that it would be rejected. I regard a lot of my work in the discussions as directed to making it acceptable. The aim was to make it possible for the student . . . to find a new kind of stability based on the acceptance of ambiguity and uncertainty.
>
> Abercrombie (1969: 171)

Yet, she argued, the 'permissive' atmosphere which enabled such acceptance developed most readily not under *laissez-faire* conditions but when the rules governing the conduct of the group were understood and accepted by all its members.

Like Foulkes, she felt that leaders, or conductors, played a crucial role in all these processes. She argued that they must be prepared, as leaders in rather than of the group, to make themselves equal members within it. So, they must exercise self-denial, listen attentively, speak little, be bound by the group's rules and be open to comment and hostility from other participants. Yet they must also be alert to the individual's or the group's need for interpretation or enquiry. She believed that through their own behaviour, teachers could offer students alternative models of the learning process. In addition, since much formal education inculcated in learners attitudes of authority-dependence, teachers had the delicate task of gradually abrogating this authority to the group, while initially using it to protect and encourage full, unfettered, active participation by every member.

Since her aims were educational, she argued that 'corrective interaction' which had learning as its aim could take place most effectively not, as Foulkes advocated for psychotherapy, in a group of strangers but among colleagues. If colleagues were involved together in reflection, experimentation and action, they were more likely to transfer what they had learnt to their work situation and to spread the possibility of further change within it. Similarly, the leader did not have to be a stranger to the group but might usefully be steeped in the problems and culture of the group, department or institution. In Nias (1989) I have explored in greater detail Foulkes's ideas, Abercrombie's adaptation of them and the use that school teachers make of small-group discussion in promoting educational change.

For thirty years after her introduction to group analysis, she acted on many occasions as a group conductor, modelling the educational uses of associative discussion and training others to adopt the alert, sensitive yet self-denying roles of peer, facilitator, interpreter and chairperson, which she combined so well. Perhaps because of this experience she also advocated support groups for group leaders which would enable them to share concerns and anxieties, pool expertise and go on learning from one another.

Part 3 begins with a lengthy extract from *Aims and Techniques of Group Teaching* (1970), because in this monograph, Abercrombie distinguished group-analytic methods and principles used for educational purposes, from other types of group method employed in higher education. She also drew distinctions between groups used for psychotherapeutic and educational ends, examined the role and potential of therapeutically oriented groups in education for the professions, summarized the pedagogical skills and challenges of using groups of any kind and considered the part which was and could be played by group teaching within the wider context of the aims of university education. The value to teachers in higher education of this broad and comprehensive account is emphasized by the fact that the monograph went through four editions by 1979. Here, I have used the earliest edition because it contains the most succinct account of Abercrombie's ideas, but I have made reference to the fourth edition (Abercrombie and Terry, 1979) when I thought that the reader might wish to be directed to further examples or a more extensive bibliography.

The remaining extracts in Part 3 illustrate the way in which Abercrombie interpreted and developed the methods and principles of 'associative' group discussion, as she worked with students in medical, architectural and teacher education and with university teachers. I have made no attempt to arrange these extracts according to themes, because each of them ranges over several interlocking issues (for example, the nature of a 'permissive' group; the role of the conductor; the levels of meaning which exist simultaneously in group discussion). The article comparing Foulkes and Escher (pp. 98–101) serves the additional purpose of stressing the visual quality of Abercrombie's thinking and the way in which she used words and illustrations to complement one another.

Teaching in Groups in Higher Education: Types, Purposes and Techniques

From *Aims and Techniques of Group Teaching*. London: Society for Research into Higher Education, 1st edn, 1970 (and 4th edn, 1979, with P.M. Terry).

The term 'group' will be used here to mean a *number of people who are in face-to-face contact, so that each of them can interact with all the others* . . . A class cannot be a group if numbers are too large for each member to be able to interact with each of the others. But nor is a small class necessarily a group, for while the class is in session the teacher may be the only person who inter-acts which each of all the others, and with whom the others interact. In group teaching in the sense in which I use it here, the teacher deliberately withdraws from being the focus of attention and his efforts are directed towards encouraging interaction among all the members: this includes himself but not as the dominating member.

To say the teacher is not 'the *dominating* member' does not lessen his importance, does not lower his status. It is necessary to be sharply explicit about this apparently simple but basic point because it is so often misunderstood, the teacher being described as neutral or passive, taking little part, and so on. The student will not perceive him so, for he is in authority, and he is an authority. (Peters's (1966) distinction between two states of authority – that of being 'in authority' and that of being 'an authority', is useful here. A teacher is 'in authority' as the representative of the educational establishment, notably he is often concerned with examinations. He is also, we trust, 'an authority' in the subject the students want to learn and in being competent to teach it to them.) Neither teacher nor student can deny this; the asymmetry is after all the basis of the contract between them. It is a different role the teacher needs to play, not a lesser one. Retaining both states of authority, he should not behave in an authoritarian, domineering manner . . .

The demand for discussion methods of teaching

The increasing recognition of the value of discussion methods, which has been apparent during the last decade, reflects the growing interest in the active processes in learning (the 'child-centred' movement in primary education prepared the way for changes in tertiary education in this respect). The lecture in which the student passively absorbs information, the teacher getting little or no feedback as to the effectiveness of his teaching, is being challenged as the main instrument of teaching. The Hale Committee on University Teaching Methods (University Grants Committee (UGC), 1964), for instance, . . . reported that teaching methods were 'all tutorial and seminar', while The National Union of Students' *Report of the Commission on Teaching in Higher Education* (1969) . . . indicated a distinct preference for small-group teaching.

The Hale Committee dealt at some length with discussion periods (by which it means tutorials and seminars) as alternatives or supplements to the lecture as the main vehicle of teaching in universities. It described the lecture as

> a teaching period occupied wholly or mainly with continuous exposition by the lecturer. Students attending it may be given some opportunity for questions or a little discussion, but in the main they have nothing to do except listen and take notes.

A discussion period requires

> much more participation from the student. For example, there may be reading and study of a paper by a student; discussion, in which students are meant to take part, of topics introduced by a member of staff or a student; a member of staff may go through essays or questions prepared by student(s); there may be discussion of *any* academic matters or problems on the initiative of students or staff.

The Committee drew some distinctions between the two kinds of discussion period. A 'tutorial' was defined as a discussion period which (a) is attended by not more than four students and (b) is one of a series of such periods conducted by the same teacher; and a 'seminar' was defined as a discussion period which is not tutorial. Qualitative differences between the two kinds of discussion period were recognized, the tutorial being student-centred, the seminar subject-centred . . .

Important though the Hale Committee's findings were in stimulating thought about the need for more discussion periods in university teaching, the understanding of the potentialities of this method was limited. It seems that it was thought of as teaching the same sort of thing as could be learned from lectures or reading. To quote [Abercrombie's emphasis in all cases]:

The limitations of teaching in discussion periods, as seen by a number of universities, may be summarized as follows. It is extravagant of staff time *to do in small groups anything that could equally well be done by a lecture to a larger audience.* Moreover, the discussion group, being in its nature subject to interruptions and digressions, is not suitable for logical exposition. It moves too slowly to cover anything but a limited topic. It is also liable to suffer from incoherence, and may be damaged by any lack of balance in the opening paper.

Or again:

A lecture should be better prepared, more profound and better thought out than what is said in discussion, where the teacher is often *replying to a student's question,* so that what he says is necessarily extempore. A lecture can cover more ground than a tutorial or seminar, which is most effective when confined to *a limited topic.* It is also argued that discussion can only become effective when the student has *acquired sufficient knowledge* on which to base his contribution.

The main benefit, it seems, is to activate the student to learn:

If students are to derive full benefit from a discussion period, whether seminar or tutorial, it is essential that they should do some work beforehand on the subject to be discussed. Perhaps the most *effective way of getting students to do preparatory work* is to set them an essay or other written exercise to be prepared for discussion.

And:

We sometimes fear that the enthusiasm of many students for more teaching by discussion is derived from the expectation that it will save them trouble and make things easy. Such expectations should be disappointed. It is no kindness to a student to relieve him of the intellectual effort without which he cannot get the benefit he should from a university course. The introduction of more teaching by discussion is beneficial only when it can be matched by a corresponding increase in the amount of private study done by the student . . . Teaching by discussion, rightly used, is a *way of making the student do for himself what is too often done for him,* and if it is used in this way we do not think that it should be unduly expensive or burdensome on staff.

The advocates of this kind of discussion seem to be concerned mostly with facilitating the learning of a body of factual knowledge and generalizations. While not in the least wishing to belittle the importance of this kind of learning, opportunity for much besides can be given in various kinds of discussion groups . . .

I hope the manifold potentialities of group teaching will become clear in the discussions of varieties of group work that follow, but first I would like to elaborate further on the main differences between the assumptions underlying group teaching and the more traditional methods. It will be convenient to concentrate attention on the lecture and tutorial, for semi-nars are of a more heterogeneous category, some being examples of group work in the sense in which I am using it, others having more of the characteristics of lectures but given to a smaller number and in a less formal situation, and sometimes by people, e.g. research workers or postgraduate students, whose skill in lecturing is allegedly weaker than that of those who by title can be supposed to be good at it.

Lecture, tutorial and group compared

The group situation for learning differs markedly from teaching arrange-ments which treat the student as an individual, learning in isolation from other learners. Reading a book, or listening to a lecture, the learner is re-ceiving information from a single source. Though other students may be sitting beside him, intellectual interaction between them is reduced to a minimum, and interaction of any sort must not block the single channel through which information is piped to each from the fountainhead. It is true that a received opinion about higher education is that students learn a lot from each other; indeed, it is in order to provide extra opportunities for this that residence in college, hall or hostel is so warmly advocated. But it is not so much the intellectual substance of the curriculum that is sup-posed to be better learnt this way, but rather the social or cultural aspects of education. The teacher makes a scholar of his pupil and if other pupils make a man of him, so much the better.

In the lecture system, teaching time is devoted almost entirely to the presentation of information by the teacher. The Hale Committee (UGC, 1964) reported that students were critical of the lecture as a method of teaching because it was a 'one-way' process. It is assumed that all students have the same needs and that what is given out is received in the form in which it was intended. The students are passive recipients of information; communication is one-way – the teacher talks and the students listen. The same applies to that other major source of information, the written word, but in reading at least the student can pace himself and can go back again over difficult passages.

By contrast, in the tutorial system, teaching time is devoted to the discussion of individual students' academic work. This demands activity on the part of the student, and recognizes that he is a selective filter, that he has difficulties of attentiveness, receptivity or understanding which make it unlikely that he will, in fact, take in all the information to which he is exposed in the form intended. In a tutorial, therefore, the teacher attempts to discover and remove these blocks by listening to the student's questions and comments on what he has learned from lectures or reading. It is re-cognized that no two students are exactly alike and that the maximum benefit is gained if only one or two students are present at a time so that the teacher can give full attention to individual differences. Communication is two-way, from teacher to student, and student to teacher. In most tutorial situations (even if only two students are present), the main intentional communications take this form. There is little designed interaction between the students, though all can witness what takes place and benefit from the individual-oriented teaching directed at any one of them.

The group system of teaching focuses attention on the interaction between all participants, students and teachers, not on the polarized interaction of a student with a teacher. Like the tutorial, it recognizes individual differences, but goes further and not only allows for these differences, but actually exploits them. Exposed to the same display of information, each student has taken in not only different amounts, but different interpretations, and each learns by comparing and contrasting his uptake with that achieved by his peers. There is a network of communication between all members. In the tutorial, the students' omissions and mistakes are corrected by the teacher; if the teacher is good, the student's store of information tends to match his teacher's in both content and organization. In the group system, the student discovers his strengths and weaknesses himself as he sees his behaviour in the light of others', and he modifies his attitudes or strategies as he sees that there are as many alternatives to them as there are members of the group.

Both the individual-oriented lecture and tutorial systems tend to perpetuate the authority-dependency relationship. Although an aim of the tutorial is to encourage students to think independently, its authoritarian overtones can be seen in the clear statement made by the Franks Report [Oxford University, 1966; original emphasis]:

> At its heart is a theory of teaching young men and women to think for themselves. The undergraduate is *sent* off to forage for himself among a long list of books and journals and to produce a coherent exposition of his ideas on the subject set. The essay or prepared work is then read by its author and *criticized* by the tutor. In this discussion the undergraduate should benefit by struggling to *defend* the positions he has taken, by realizing the implications of this argument, and by glimpsing the context in which a more experienced scholar sees his problem. This process can succeed only when the tutor takes undergraduates singly, or in pairs . . . If in any group one pupil has written an essay and one or two others merely listen and perhaps throw in an occasional opinion, they are not experiencing a tutorial, but merely attending a class. For the tutorial means that the undergraduate has to try his hand at creation *under correction.*

Students' feelings about what happens in tutorials reflect this attitude of tutors. Table XX of the National Union of Students (1969) report lists eight major functions of the tutorial, as seen by students. Of these, 'To provide an opportunity for you to *consult* your tutor on work or other matters' comes first (55.3%) and 'To provide an opportunity for detailed *criticism* of your prepared work' comes second (50.6%), but 'To permit greater intellectual *give and take* between tutor and yourself' comes bottom of the list (25.5%)

[Abercrombie's emphasis]. The group system aims to emancipate the student from the authority-dependency relationship, and to help him to develop intellectual independence and maturity through interaction with peers, by glimpsing 'the various contexts in which several equals see the problem'. This aim is not seen as having high priority even in seminar teaching, according to Table XV of the NUS (1969) report which shows what respondents thought were the major functions of the seminar. Of twelve functions, 'To encourage learning and to facilitate the exchange of ideas' comes top of the list (50.4%); 'To produce greater staff–student contact' fifth (35.5%); 'To produce greater contact between participating students' eighth (25.0%), and 'To train students to work independently' tenth (17.2%).

I am certainly not suggesting that group work should replace other teaching methods, all of which have their specific values. In particular, it may well be extremely important that students should experience an expert's ways of thinking and behaving, in so far as they are demonstrated in lectures or tutorials, and should be able to incorporate a teacher's attitudes and values. I am suggesting that some varieties of group teaching can be used to achieve specific objectives and, in specific contexts, to add to the effectiveness of the total learning experience.

In organizing group work, we take note of two biological facts – that man is essentially a social animal and that he has to undergo an exceptionally long period of development. He begins life very small and helpless and for several years the difference in physical size and strength between the child and the adults who care for him is very great. In the kind of single-family home in which most children in this country grow up, the parents may seem absolute in power and authority. They are not challenged in daily contact by the hearth or at table by other adults, by people of their own generation or the grandparents' generation, as they may be in more primitive (and perhaps socially more healthy) conditions. Moreover, in small families there will be only children and adults, with nobody in between. At school, parents are replaced by teachers. Teachers too are not customarily seen to be challenged by other adults and, again, there is nobody intermediate in age between children and adults. The gulf between the generations tends to be maintained, for the children may be kept in classes of agemates (though this rigid stratification is being broken down in some schools). The increasing span of full-time education prolongs the time during which, however big and strong he is physically, the student is inferior in knowledge. The more the teachers and the institution are to be admired and respected for scholarship, the more inferior the student may feel. In addition, at university, although teachers freely admit (indeed, many parade with a didactic fervour) their own ignorance and limitations, their power, as the student sees it, is reinforced by their role as his assessors and examiners. Especially now that it is more usual for teachers deliberately to foster a non-authoritarian relationship, it is important to recognize that . . . the distance between student and teacher is much greater when seen from the standpoint

of the student than from that of the teacher, for time anticipated is vastly
longer than time experienced.

In times of ideological, technological and social stability, there may be
not much harm in this prolonged dependence of the rising generation, but
it offers two sources of difficulty in a time of rapid change. In the first place,
if the student receives a body of knowledge from what seems to be a remote
and monolithic source and swallows it whole in a childlike way, he is less
likely to question it, less likely to be able to modify it and replace it as need
arises, than if he has received it as a mature person, from a challengeable
equal. He will not feel the need to question, assess or judge if all this has
been done for him much better, as it seems to him, than he could do it,
by superiors of unquestioned wisdom. So his own powers of discrimination
cannot mature. Secondly, if he is fixed in the habit of learning only from
authority figures remote in age, he will find it more difficult to continue to
learn later in life . . . Learning in groups helps the student to share both
ignorance and knowledge with his peers and prepares him for a flexible
attitude to the roles he needs to play in teaching and learning throughout
life.

Within the general framework of educating for maturing and change,
groups can be organized in many different ways to serve different purposes.
In education, as in real life, groups will be structured, or will structure themselves according to what they expect to do, a committee differently from
a sherry party. Some groups may be organized to help students to master
the substance of the curriculum, the body of information and skills which
can be tested in examinations. Others may have the more diffuse objectives of developing effective attitudes to the subject or profession or, in
extreme cases, of changing the personality through self-knowledge. At one
end of a spectrum are groups whose main aim is to help the student to
learn a 'subject'; at the other, to help him to learn how to continue to
learn . . . A close study of such extreme positions will enlarge our understanding of the contributions that group work could make to education.
Having achieved some clarification of aims, we can bring the extremes
together more fruitfully, for they are certainly not mutually exclusive. If
helping the student to learn a subject, *in such a way* that he also learns how
to continue to learn, is an acceptable general aim of university teaching, we
can then ask what parts group work of different kinds can play, along with
other teaching methods. As we have been comparing group teaching with
lecturing and tutoring, which are concerned mostly with transmitting and
understanding 'factual' information and concepts or generalizations, we
will begin with discussing the organization of group teaching for the same
purposes.

Understanding a body of knowledge

The question is often asked whether 'factual material' can be economically
learnt in small groups. Group teaching tends to be thought of as an

alternative to the lecture and, as such, it is often said (by teachers) to be relatively inefficient because not nearly so much ground can be covered in an hour's discussion as in a lecture. This objection is valid only if what the lecturer covers in an hour is as well understood by the students as by the teacher, which is rarely the case. It is easy for a lecturer to over-estimate grossly the amount of information that students understand and retain from the lecture which he worked so hard at, organized so clearly and delivered with such lucidity, precision, punch and charm. Therefore, in considering the economy, in terms of manpower and time, of learning facts, concepts and generalizations, group teaching should be compared with seminars and tutorials rather than with lectures; it should be used as a complement to learning from books or from the lecturer's spoken word, rather than as a substitute for these. There is little danger that lectures will be abandoned; as the Hale Committee (UGC, 1964) reports:

> the overwhelming weight of university opinion is that lectures have an essential function, particularly for opening up a subject for students who are not in a position to do it for themselves by unassisted reading, and also for giving more detailed information where suitable text-books are lacking. Lectures have certain advantages over discussion periods in that continuous exposition, free from interruptions, can be better prepared and more profound than teaching in a discussion period, can cover more ground, and can enable an inspiring teacher to in-fluence more students.

The great advantage of group work is in facilitating the understanding, as distinct from mere acceptance, of information – in helping the student to comprehend it, grasp it, make it his own. A simple way of applying group work to a lecture is to invite questions and comments at the end of it from a group, not from individuals. However, this does not meet the need to deal with students' difficulties of assimilation, because usually their misunder-standings are not obvious to them . . . It is only people who are reasonably sophisticated who can ask reasonable (that is, answerable) questions. They must also be self-confident enough to be able to make a confession of ignorance and confusion. A more useful way of ensuring understanding of a lecture is to form 'buzz groups'. This can be simply done by asking four or five people in a row to turn round and talk with an equal number in the row behind for a few minutes about the main issues raised. Each group frames questions and comments which are then put to the lecturer.

It must be recognized, however, that the spatial arrangements of most lecture theatres are designed to concentrate all the attention of members of the audience on the speaker and to prevent interaction among themselves. The lecturer is the only person who can see everybody and whom all the others can see. During the conventional hour or fifty minutes he is the only person who should speak; it is discourteous to the lecturer, and to the class, for any one else to speak, or for another to listen if he does so. No amount of trendy informality on the part of the lecturer – of using the bench to sit on and swing legs from, instead of to stand behind – can loosen the barriers to communication that are imposed by straight rows of fixed seats. The arrangements at the Law School in Sydney should facilitate interaction at times when it will be beneficial, while retaining the advantages of the po-larized orientation necessary when focusing attention on the lecturer, or looking at slides or other demonstration material. The seats are arranged in concentric semi-elipses, each row slightly raised above the last, the lec-ture bench being on the minor diameter. Each seat, a comfortable bucket chair, swivels and swings easily on a steel arm, so that its occupant can as conveniently face someone sitting behind him as one sitting opposite; and these changes of orientation through 290 degrees are made as quickly and smoothly as those made through less than half a circle with eye and neck movements. The furniture arrangements thus symbolize and facilitate inter-action between all members of the assembly.

Innumerable varieties of group, differing from seminars in the extent to which interaction among students is encouraged, can be organized outside the lecture theatre to discuss the substance of a lecture or of notes specially prepared by the teacher, of a published article or a chapter in a textbook. One of my colleagues, Turlogh O'Brien, a chemist, developed the following method for teaching a course on 'materials' to students of architecture. The class of 36 students was divided into three groups, recent performance in examinations being used to ensure that each group sampled the whole academic range of the class. Each week, a set of typescript notes such as could have been the summary of an hour's lecture was given to each stu-dent and one hour was set aside for the study of these. After individual study of the notes, each group met to discuss them for an hour or so, working under a student chairman who had been nominated (in rotation) the previous week. During this period, the teacher wandered from one group to another, to clear up any points that could be dealt with briefly. Then all three groups met for half an hour to report and raise major issues. Students found this a convenient and stimulating way of learning difficult material. They became familiar with a new technical vocabulary as they bandied the words about and got a sounder grasp of new concepts by manipulating them, rephrasing them and learning to see their implications. The clever ones said that points they thought they had understood quite well in their individual reading appeared more clearly, or in a different light, in discussion. The less adept commented that it helped their morale to find that other students had not correctly understood parts of the text and that even the most competent ones had not grasped the whole of it.

Erskine and Tomkin (1963) used discussions in groups of twelve students as part of a carefully planned method for teaching topographical anatomy (which, as they say, is a 'formidably descriptive science'). Two hours of discussion among twelve students with one teacher replaced nine hours of lectures. The authors emphasized the importance of planned preparation for the discussion periods; active learning was encouraged and themes were chosen for discussion that would help to organize seemingly unconnected facts into a meaningful pattern. They report that the results as evaluated by objective tests, standardized viva voce examinations and essay-type questions were decisively better than those of conventional teaching methods. [For further details, see Abercrombie and Terry, 1979.]

Other approaches aim not only to ensure that 'facts' and 'concepts' are well understood, but that general attitudes to the subject matter are changed in a desirable direction. An important experiment in teaching psychiatry to medical students has been described by Walton (1968) who made a comparison between students taught by lecture and clinical demonstrations to the whole class, and those taught in groups of twelve. Students taught by lecture did not learn more 'facts' than those taught in groups, and they did equally well in tests of clinical skill, but they did not change so much (in a favourable direction) in attitudes to psychiatry. Students taught in groups judged their training as superior, feeling more confident in their own skills, and more interested in psychiatric patients.

An approach to teaching graduates in a course on the theory of education is described by Nisbet (1966). The aim was to introduce the students to 'profound, comprehensive and critical examination' of fundamental principles and values. Each of a group of eight students chose a topic on which he could make a contribution, and took it in turns to develop this at two successive meetings. At the first of his two meetings, the student produced 'six statements worth making' about his topic, taking about twenty minutes to introduce them. At a second meeting the statements were gone over in an atmosphere of discipline, decision and urgency, the members committing themselves to agreement or disagreement. Minutes of the two meetings were produced at the next meeting, followed by the beginning of the next student's cycle. This method provides experience of selecting material, of adapting discussion to different atmospheres and of behaving as is appropriate in committees. [For further details, see Abercrombie and Terry, 1979.]

Syndicate work

In this kind of group work, which has been much used in training for management, the group works together for meetings, in the absence, or only occasional presence of the tutor, and co-operates in producing a report or in making decisions. The emphasis is on interaction between members and decreased dependence on the teacher. Teaching by the syndicate method has been mostly used with graduates, but similar approaches could surely be effectively made with undergraduates. Collier discusses the potentialities of this method and includes a detailed description of his use of it in his thought-provoking book *New Dimensions in Higher Education* (1968). Earlier (1966) he reported an extremely interesting experiment on encouraging students to think for themselves about an academic subject. He was conducting a course on educational sociology, for a class of 40 teachers working for master's degrees. The course was concerned with five major concepts, such as social class differentiation in Western societies or planning for change and innovation. The class was divided into small groups or syndicates of five or six students who carried out assignments based on reading, discussion and writing. Some of the assignments resulted in reports and the teacher would summarize these in a lecture, correcting misconceptions or filling in gaps – doing, it would seem, to the group product what a tutor does to an individual's. The experiment is outstanding in its clear statement of objectives combined with sensitivity to the non-cognitive elements in a teaching situation . . .

Collier (1969) also reports further on the syndicate method. He emphasizes that its distinctive characteristic is the uniting of considerable independence for the groups with a systematic course of study. He suggests that it may have special significance for inter-disciplinary courses. [For further details, see Abercrombie and Terry, 1979.]

Learning to assess one's own work

A consequence of prolonging full-time education is that the student is unable to measure his achievements by testing his behaviour in the real world. The embryo writer, for instance, is not assessed by the readers he would address and his only yardstick is his teachers' opinion. Architectural students, in particular, are completely cut off from reality-testing. An important part of their education takes place in the studio. The student is set a series of design tasks which may take a few hours, days, weeks or even months. His work ends in the production of a set of drawings or models, and the buildings they represent will never be tested by weather or use or public taste. At the end of each project the student's designs are criticized by a group of experts, including his own teachers, perhaps teachers from other schools, professional architects and often other students . . . Only to the extent the individual student can understand, evaluate and take to heart their criticisms, can he learn to make better designs. His teacher's judgement must be taken on trust.

We have tried to tackle the problem of helping students to develop their own powers of continuously judging their work in progress by organizing 'self-assessing' groups. In each group the students examine each other's designs: they are encouraged to try to understand rather than to criticize in the adverse sense. This stimulates a student to be analytically interested in solutions other than his own, gives him practice in sorting out main principles and puts him in a more mature relationship to work, both his own and others', than when he listens only to the criticisms of experts. This process of mutual assessment may take an hour or two. At the end of it, each group presents a report to the whole class. The teachers may comment, fill in gaps or summarize; they do not need to deal with details, but can restrict their remarks to generalizations. Because the students have already worked at understanding the designs, they can much better understand the teachers' comments. The whole procedure is designed to increase the active participation of the students in assessment.

In the present climate of dissatisfaction with and distrust of the whole system of examinations, whether for entrance to secondary education or to a profession, it is essential that we reconsider the role of assessment in education. Given a sound educational environment in which collaboration in the learning task is based on mutual respect, and competitiveness is not destructive, red in tooth and claw, but a spice that enhances individual differences, assessment by students of their own and others' work can be well integrated into the educational process.

In the kinds of group work to be discussed next, the aim moves still further away from that of facilitating the intake and comprehension of a body of facts and generalizations and towards the aim of enabling the student to modify his behaviour in specific directions by examining it and learning to understand from it. Group work of this kind tends to use some of the ideas and techniques of psychotherapy and at this point it may be helpful to diverge a little and discuss the relationships between teaching and psychotherapy.

Teaching and psychotherapy

Teachers and psychotherapists both aim to change behaviour; they are people who have been trained in special skills and who are given special opportunities to exercise them in helping other people to behave in the future in certain prescribed situations in certain ways which they otherwise would not do. In teaching it is supposed that the recipient (pupil) has not yet learned how to behave in the required way because of youth or ignorance – so a child who cannot yet read may be helped to learn to do so. In psychotherapy it is supposed that the recipient (patient) has already learned habits that are bad and consequently he must develop different reactions to the same situations; he has to *un*learn and *re*learn. [For further details, see Abercrombie and Terry, 1979.]

Teachers and psychotherapists differ in that teachers work with pupils who by and large are mentally like themselves, except that they are ignorant of a more or less prescribed field of knowledge in which the teacher is expert. By contrast, psychotherapists work with patients, people whose mental outlook is maladapted to life.

The same piece of information can, in some circumstances, be taught didactically while, in other circumstances, a therapeutic approach is necessary. A modern schoolchild has no difficulty in learning that the Earth is a sphere and goes round the Sun, but there was a time when the idea was unlearnable, indeed was actively rejected, by quite clever adults. They had very good reasons for being unable to learn it, because it ran counter to their other beliefs. They could not take it in until they had *unlearned* other and contrary ways of thinking. Learning anything that is new to the world must involve some unlearning, since our knowledge tends to form an integrated, consistent whole, and a lot of more or less relevant parts of it will have to modified if a new piece of information is to be incorporated (see Abercrombie, 1960, for elaboration of this).

The newer the behaviour is, and the more complicated and subtle the change of behaviour aimed at, the more likely that a psychotherapeutic approach rather than a didactic one will be effective. Conventional teaching works at the mental level of conscious, rational behaviour; psychotherapy attempts to help people to behave more rationally by making them aware of unconscious or preconscious processes that cause them to behave irrationally.

I believe that certain kinds of group discussion can provide opportunities for such 'psychological exploration'. This is not to be confused with the possible cathartic effects of small-group teaching. Although undoubtedly emotions play an important role in learning, 'letting off steam' is not always conducive to rational thought. I believe that many of the difficulties of thinking clearly can be approached through reasoning in a permissive atmosphere which encourages exploration. In the variety of group work described next, the aim is to help students to become aware, by personal interaction, of their habitual ways of thinking and behaving and to modify them if it seems desirable.

'Free' or 'associative' group discussion for training in observation and reasoning

[In Abercrombie and Terry (1979), Abercrombie writes: 'The technique was at first described as "free" group discussion but this gave rise to some misunderstanding about its nature, so I now prefer to call it "associative" group discussion.' I have used the later title for Part Three.]

A technique which incorporates some of the principles of group-analytic psychotherapy (Foulkes and Anthony, 1965; Foulkes, 1964), was developed by the author in an attempt to help preclinical medical students to observe accurately and comprehensively and to draw reasonable conclusions from their observations. The method has been described at some length in Abercrombie, 1960 [in this volume, see pp. 123–8]. Barnett (1958) too adopted this approach, using 'free group discussion' in a class on human biology. He reported that students who displayed an emotional bias in discussing an excerpt from an essay on control experiments 'were *eventually* corrected *by other students*, as the latter *gradually* formulated their thoughts on the subject during *uncontrolled* discussion', the emphasized words indicating respects in which 'free group discussion' differs from the ordinary seminar. [For further details, see Abercrombie and Terry, 1979.]

'Free' or 'associative' group discussion and the professional role

An opportunity to attempt similar work on a much shorter time-scale arose during a recent visit to Australia, when the author was invited by the Department of Education at Sydney University to conduct five discussions with a group of ten Diploma of Education students who had volunteered to join this experiment. This series of discussions was intended to give participants an opportunity to explore the sort of feelings that they, as teachers in training, might have about the professional role they were preparing to adopt, and thereby to help them to come to terms with the changes in self-perception that are necessary if they are to switch roles effectively, from being pupils to being teachers. After having set the scene by describing very briefly my own interest in this emancipating kind of teaching, I said very little during the discussions. The chief points I brought to the group's notice are given in the summary which follows.

In the first meeting we talked about submission (each student had contributed a word that he would like to discuss, and this one was chosen; it was significant that other contributions – authority, leadership, discipline, ambition, power, success, criticism – were also relevant to the classroom situation). The first topic raised was submission to conscription for the Vietnam war and the students continued to talk from the viewpoint of those who submit, rather than those who are submitted to, behaving as pupils rather than as teachers. For the second meeting they decided to talk about the problems of being a teacher. One student started off by telling how bad the lesson was that she had attended yesterday; but, she asked despairingly, would she be able to do any better when she was faced with a class? The talk moved away from the difficulty of the teacher–pupil relationship to matters they felt were beyond their control, the difficulties of 'the system'. There was little money; equipment and buildings were bad. The children might be naughty or stupid. Parents were demanding or apathetic. A headmistress who persecuted her staff was cited – you'd get the sack if you criticized. One pronounced that all education is politics; the only way to change it is through political action. Towards the end they came back to personal relationships in the classroom, when one student talked of her embarrassment at discussing four-letter words with the boys.

For the third seminar the students decided to discuss control of the class. The effect of the teacher's personality was emphasized, and they cited examples from their own experience of being taught both at school and at university. The importance of engaging the interest of the children was discussed, but throughout the belief was expressed that the children must not be let loose – you had to know what they were all doing. I related this attitude to their own complaints of the Diploma course, which they felt to be rigid and repressive . . .

The students did not want any agenda for the last two meetings, a sign that they had accepted the principle of free group discussion. The first part of the last discussion was concerned mostly with frank criticism of the Diploma of Education course, but there was a constructive theme running through it. Some of the students were arranging a series of meetings which aimed at reorganizing the course; even if they could not achieve anything for themselves, it would help the succeeding class, they said. It was notable how their perception of authority figures changed during the discussion. At first it appeared that no improvements could be made unless all their bad teachers were removed and the whole structure scrapped; but later, examples were cited of bad teachers who turned out to be approachable (though with difficulty) and who had responded well to students' criticisms. Parents at first were described as interfering or threatening; but later, it seemed, some might be quite nice to know and it might be possible to collaborate with them in the child's interests. A lively and touching description was given of a grandfather and granddaughter working together on new maths. There seemed a marked change in self-perception since the first discussion, which had been dominated by feelings of impotence, and of the impossibility of doing useful work because of the difficulties imposed by the political and administrative set-up, both in schools and in the Diploma course. Now they could entertain the possibility that individuals could take initiatives, and could effectively collaborate with each other and with members of the older generation.

It might be expected that the taking on of the professional role would be more difficult for teachers than for most others, for it involves a complete reversal, and not only a modification, of the perception of the self in the teaching–learning relationship. It is not surprising that many students get upset by these taxing demands . . . It is fortunate that one of the most lucid and sensitive reports of group teaching is one with teachers in training (Richardson, 1967) which is discussed below.

A variation of free group discussion has been used with postgraduate students of architecture who were preparing for the final professional qualification (Abercrombie, *et al.*, 1970; in this volume, see pp. 135–43). The whole year's teaching was oriented towards self-education, and the aim of the discussions was to help students with the problems of being educated for change . . .

Later, as part of a project supported by the University Grants Committee on improving small group teaching in the universities, Abercrombie and Terry (1978a) conducted discussions among teachers of different disciplines and institutions about their concerns with current group work. It became clear that their behaviour as teachers was strongly influenced by such intangibles as the conflicts between different aspects of themselves – the academic and personal, their motivations for taking up the profession, and their own problems as well as their students' over the authority-dependency relationship. In comparison and contrast with others, each participant could question how his attitudes might be modified to achieve the objects he desired in his teaching. Free or associative discussion in this case, though initially focused on small-group teaching, was helping to subserve staff development more generally (Abercrombie, 1977b; in this volume see pp. 103–11).

Training in human relations

Attempts are being made to apply to university teaching some of the ideas and methods of therapeutically oriented group work which have been developed for training managers, social workers and others in human relations. This trend is strong in the USA, and one of the most influential methods is the so-called T- (Training) group, sensitivity training, group dynamics or group relations training. This approach to re-education has developed from work by the National Training Laboratory in Group Development at Bethel, Maine, USA, beginning in 1947. A good account of it is given by Bradford *et al.* (1964), and an excellent brief introduction to it by Smith (1969). An essential characteristic of this type of training is that a considerable amount of time is spent by members of the course talking about their relationship with each other. By talking specifically about one another's behaviour they avoid being too abstract, and they learn from their own experience, rather than by being taught . . . Participants are helped to diagnose their own behaviour and experiment with it in an environment specially designed for this purpose. The T-group is a specially organized group, in which each participant may learn about his own motives, feelings and strategies in dealing with others, and about the reactions of others to him. Although resembling therapy groups in some respects, it differs in that the participants are not patients; it deals with present rather than past behaviour, and conscious and preconscious rather than unconscious processes. T-groups sometimes take place in a training laboratory, a temporary residential community dedicated to the stimulation and support of experimental learning and change. Help is provided in applying the new ways of behaving which have been learnt in the protected environment of the laboratory to real-life situations. [For further details, see Abercrombie and Terry, 1979.] . . . In Britain the Tavistock Institute of Human Relations has applied group techniques to various kinds of training (see, for instance, Gosling *et al.*, 1967) and has influenced some university teachers. [For further details, see Abercrombie and Terry, 1979.]

The work of Richardson (1967) has been inspired by that of the Tavistock Institute . . . Essentially this kind of group work consists in enabling members of a group to study the conscious and unconscious motivations that affect behaviour in the group. The aim of Richardson's teaching was to help the students to develop a greater understanding of themselves as persons interacting with others, and more specifically, with their future pupils. In her book *Group Study for Teachers* (1967) she describes with great insight the behaviour in differently organized groups in a postgraduate course on education. One kind of tutorial, dealing with educational issues, worked within the accepted framework of tutorial groups, but she gave students the responsibility for planning and implementing their work themselves. This faced them with problems of their relation to the teacher and the nature of authority. Other group meetings, 'voluntary study groups', were of a much more experimental kind and in them the aim of the group was to study itself. She discusses students' complicated reactions to assessment of their work and all that this implies for their relation to their studies, and to the fact that her teaching was experimental or research-oriented. She describes the importance of furniture arrangement in the classroom, and the symbolic value of being late for classes, or absent. It is impossible to do justice to this work in summary; it should be studied carefully by anyone interested in group work. [For further details of work with social workers, teachers and medical teachers, see Abercrombie and Terry, 1979.]

Promising though the therapeutic approach might seem to be for students who are going to deal with human relations professionally, its incorporation into academic work is undoubtedly full of difficulties. A particularly interesting situation arises when medical students are learning about psychiatry and especially psychotherapy. Here the tendency for group discussion to merge into group psychotherapy becomes strong, partly because the teachers may themselves be psychotherapists, and partly because the topic itself is likely to resonate with the students' natural anxieties about their own mental health. Seguin (1965), for instance, reports on an ambitious programme of group teaching in psychological medicine, an area in which surely an understanding of one's own behaviour is relevant. Lectures were reduced, and groups of twenty students discussed the themes in seminars; clinical groups of five included in their discussion their reactions and feelings when interviewing a patient. Each student was also assigned to a 'working group' of ten, which met weekly throughout the academic year, and was intended to continue through the five-year course. The purpose of the working groups was to help students to understand themselves and to allow them to experience in their own reactions the psychological mechanisms they had been taught about. Each student was asked to give an autobiography, and a report on his impressions in the dissecting room. As might be expected, the seminars proved most successful, and the working groups most difficult. The students in the working groups were aggressive and hostile and the rather strongly therapeutically oriented technique was changed in the second year, less emphasis being given to personal problems, with encouraging results. [For further details, see Abercrombie and Terry, 1979.]

The violence of reaction which often occurs when therapeutic techniques are introduced into academic work may be a transient phenomenon which will disappear when attitudes to mental health become more sophisticated. Until then, even in the teaching of psychiatry itself, therapeutic skills must be tempered if the student is to benefit from this unconventional approach to learning. He has come (overtly, at any rate) to get enlightenment on other people's psychopathology, not his own, and may not see, nor wish to see, how closely the two interact. At present, I agree with Morris (1965) who in a wise essay on learning in groups remarks that

experiences of psychoanalytically oriented group work can be powerfully illuminating but the methods used by the group leader in these
situations do not provide themselves an actual model of how to conduct groups in other quite different circumstances . . .

Team work

Team work, which results in a more or less tangible end product, or at least
has an easily understood aim, obviously requires good interaction between
participants, and the actual practice of it can be used to improve skills in
interpersonal relationships. This sort of group work is probably one of the
most conventional, most easily understood and most successfully exploited.
It is the kind of thing students spontaneously organize themselves – in, for
instance, Union affairs, arranging a debate, a cricket match, a play, a
magazine. They set themselves a socially acceptable and clearly understood
task. Their success in organizing teamwork is measured by the success of
the product, but whether or not they succeed in the declared task, they will
have learnt a great deal about human interaction while doing it. Team work
can, however, be arranged so that learning about team work is the major
aim and the achievement of the tangible end product is only a secondary
one, an acceptable vehicle.

Ability to work effectively in teams is increasingly important to many
professions – medicine, dentistry, engineering, architecture . . . We have
undertaken some forms of teaching which we hope will help students to
come to terms with the need for the very profound change in attitude
which is necessary if they are to meet the demands of current practice
(Abercrombie, 1967; in this volume, see pp. 129–43). [For further details
see Abercrombie and Terry, 1979.]

We turn, finally, to the use of groups for encouraging originality or
creativity. This is possibly the least conventional use of groups, for commonly it is thought that the production of new ideas is an extremely individual matter, and that work in groups tends to become rather neutral or
pedestrian. In certain circumstances, however, it seems that some people
can be more original or innovative as a result of interaction in a group than
they are when working alone.

Groups for developing creativity

'Brain-storming' and 'synectics' are methods for producing original ideas in
groups. In brain-storming (Osborn, 1953) the group is encouraged to be as
spontaneous as possible in making suggestions about the solution of a given
problem. Quite wild contributions are offered, and criticism must be
withheld. Different ideas combine together to make a new and creative
solution.

'Synectics' is a more sophisticated technique developed by Gordon (1961) and his associates. The term 'synectics', meaning the joining together of different and apparently irrelevant elements, applies to the integration of diverse individuals into a problem-stating and problem-solving group. The problems tackled are often technical ones set by industry – such as how to make a self-sealing toothpaste tube – and the aim is not only to solve such problems, but also to train participants to be more creative in so doing.

People of very diverse backgrounds are chosen to form a group of five or six which may work together for several sessions, and great care is taken in selecting the participants. A biologist and an actor may be included in a group working on a chemical problem, for instance, because it is believed that analogical ways of thinking are important in creative work, and that the different kinds of analogies used in various disciplines, other than that of the technology directly relating to the problem, are helpful. A great deal of the work is done by discussion, but model-making and other practical exercises may be undertaken. Members must be willing to function on a more or less non-rational basis; a well-trained group, it is said, can

compress into a few hours the kind of semiconscious mental activity which might take months of incubation for a single person . . . Non-rational communication . . . produces evocative metaphors, images with rough surfaces and fissures on which others can get a grip and participate. Of course, this kind of non-rational interplay is only part of a process which spirals up towards increasing coherence. Ultimate solutions to problems are rational; the process of finding them is not.

The proponents of synectics believe that creative efficiency in people can be markedly increased if they understand the psychological processes by which they operate; that the emotional component of the creative process is more important than the intellectual, the irrational more important than the rational; and that it is these emotional, irrational elements which can and must be understood in order to increase the probability of success in a problem-solving situation. Great efforts are made, therefore, to help the participants to become aware of their own mental processes; and verbalization of thoughts and feelings is encouraged. Attention is paid to such intangibles as group climate.

In spite of its insistence on the irrational, on playfulness, on the need for paying attention to the commonplace and to apparent irrelevancies, this is a highly intellectual and rigorous technique. The approach has a great deal to offer to education, and Gordon's book, with its lively descriptions of 'synectic' group experiences, merits careful study.

In an anecdotal essay on the relation of group activity to creativity in science, Abelson (1965) makes many points of great interest to group workers generally. A working group can provide a micro-climate which gives intellectual satisfaction, support in time of difficulty, and opportunities for sharpening judgement and correcting 'blind spots'. Abelson believes that a research group works best if its members differ in background, temperament and special skills and knowledge. Each member must receive so many benefits from the association that self-interest is best served by the smooth running of the group. He distinguishes this sort of association between intellectual equals from team work in which the juniors who are just 'so many pairs of hands' have no opportunity to be creative; indeed, innovation on their part might be detrimental to the team effort. Abelson is well aware of many non-cognitive factors involved in scientific work: individuals may have seasonal variations in creativeness which need to be taken into account in planning; the value of deadlines in stimulating bursts of exceptional activity; the sensitivity of groups to the wider environment – he gives examples of groups whose cohesiveness was apparently encouraged by being in an alien environment. There is need for many more naturalistic studies of this kind of group work in practice which will not only improve productiveness by more effective institutional organization, but also help scientists to regulate their own individual behaviour.

Evaluation of group work

As is natural with innovators, most teachers who experiment with groups attempt to evaluate them as they go along and use their own judgement of their successes to tell them whether to stop or continue. Quite often they ask the students for their opinions; often these are favourable, but this does not necessarily mean that they have learnt more of what the teacher wanted them to learn; it may be that they just like the social situation. Sometimes they are not favourable; and the more unconventional the procedure and the more deep-going the attempts to wean the student from dependency, the more likely this will be; again, this does not mean the students have or have not learned what it was hoped they would learn. Quite often my students have said, months, or even years, after a course of free group discussions, that they now understand what I was getting at; some of these had enjoyed themselves at the time and others had not. [For further details, see Abercrombie and Terry, 1979.] In making use of the findings of experiments it is, of course, very important to remember how specific the effects may be. The results of Cottrel (UGC, 1964), for instance, who investigated the effectiveness of different sizes of tutorial group in supplementing instruction by lectures in physical chemistry, might be cited as indicating that the size of a group does not matter. He found that variation in size of group from three to 24 students had no significant effect on the performance of students in an examination consisting of 34 short answer questions covering most of the ground dealt with in the lectures. However, the side-effects of the different numbers differed: the tutors found teaching groups of 24 less pleasant than smaller groups, but had the impression that personal rapport with students was gained as readily in groups of twelve as in groups of three. It could be, therefore, that some differences would be detected in the learning of different sized groups if other criteria were looked at than mere success in learning factual material.

One of the difficulties of evaluating group work is that it is easier to devise ways of measuring differences in simple responses than in the more complicated and subtle ones, whether these are side-effects or the main aims of the teaching. Such evidence as we have from students' introspection, teachers' observations and controlled experiments is encouraging, but we need a lot more information about the effects of group teaching and, as in all educational research, we need to state our objectives clearly and describe our procedures comprehensively and precisely. [For further details, see Abercrombie and Terry, 1979.]

This brief review has by no means exhausted the many possible varieties of group work that might be useful in higher education, and any teacher using group methods will find endless stimulation in developing techniques to suit his general circumstances, his varying students and his different aims.

Learning to teach in groups

Skill in group teaching needs to be cultivated, just as skill in lecturing or in tutoring . . . There has been a gratifying growth of serious interest in learning how to teach at tertiary level since in 1969 the University Grants Committee recommended each university to make arrangements for training its academic staff in teaching. Most of the courses organized to foster this include some discussion of small-group teaching. [For further details, see Abercrombie and Terry, 1979.]

There is a vast and rapidly increasing literature on behaviour in small groups (see Abercrombie, 1966, for an introduction to this) and much of it is relevant to teaching. Besides the work already referred to above, Mc-Keachie (1963) surveys a wide range of methods of student-centred teaching, including small-group discussions. A collection of essays on *The Dynamics of Instructional Groups* (Henry, 1960), though concerned with school teaching, will be found useful for those interested in higher education.

There are a few general principles about the 'group situation' which it may be useful to discuss here. The central one is that the teacher assumes a different role from the customary one. His role is to emancipate the students from dependence on him (and other authorities) as the sources of knowledge and competence, and to encourage their own maturation. It is not the aim that is unconventional – most university teachers would claim the encouragement of vigorous intellectual growth as among their objectives. It is the methods by which this is done that distinguish group work from didactic teaching . . . It is essential that the teacher should be clear about the role he intends to adopt and make it clear to students; it may take quite a long time for students to understand the unfamiliar role, and exposition of it needs to be reinforced by the teacher's behaviour. It is not unusual for teachers, swinging away from the authoritarian position of the lecturer, to adopt a *laissez-faire* attitude in a group.

In a characteristically lucid and concise article Stenhouse (1972) argues:

Successful participant small groups in education are likely to be formal rather than informal. They call for rules and conventions. Many seminars fail because tutors see them as informal occasions . . . The teacher will be most effective if he defines his role and thereby makes his use of authority also rule-governed, and his area of initiative clear. Small group work is not forwarded by the renunciation of authority, but by its definition . . . Group rules and teaching roles need to be logically consonant with the demands of an explicit task . . . and need to take account of the psychology of groups . . . The problem of developing satisfactory small group work depends as much on student training as on teacher training.

Before focusing attention on what goes on within the group room, it is important to consider the contribution that is inevitably made by what has already gone on outside it. Each student comes into the room with his particular personality, his own history and more immediate concerns; and for a shorter or longer time, these dwell in his mind, giving little room for new tenants, the ideas the teacher wants to put in. A teacher of linguistics asked an evening class of mature students what they were thinking about at the beginning of a class. It was about such things as the tedious journey to class, the hurried meal they had just eaten, or the one they were looking forward to, difficulty in arranging for a baby-sitter (Uren, 1972). On three occasions when teachers were discussing problems of group teaching and one of them was unusually silent it turned out that personal problems were on their minds. The group conductor cannot be expected to be able to deal specifically with such problems, only to be aware that they may exist, and to set the pace accordingly.

But it is not only personal problems, whether trivial or tragic, that affect the group climate. The 'group situation' occurs within an 'institutional situation', from which it cannot be hermetically sealed, nor would we wish it to be so, for we would hope that reciprocally it would affect the institutional climate. The walls of the group room form a selectively semi-permeable membrane like that which encloses the whole human body, and every cell within it. A group will get going more quickly and easily if the institutional climate is a favourable one, if it is not too syllabus- and examination-bound, not too authoritarian, paternalistic or anonymous, and not too careless of the personal needs of its students nor denigratory of their potential for autonomous learning. Even within the most adverse climates it is possible to create a micro-environment where a teacher has a small group of students all his own for several weeks together, but it takes time. [For further details, see Abercrombie and Terry, 1979.]

The physical environment in which a group meets, the comportment of the teacher and the expectations of the students are very important in group teaching. They are not more influential than in conventional teaching situations, but in the latter they are accepted, self-understood, so ritualized that people conform to them automatically and unquestioningly and in so doing ignore them. By contrast, in the present context of education the nuances of behaviour in groups are as little understood as are those of the actors in a Japanese opera by a Western audience.

As to the physical environment, it is extraordinary how few rooms in a university building are really suitable for group discussion: 'There was much complaint about accommodation for teaching by tutorial or seminar', the Hale Committee (UGC, 1964) reports. It is extraordinary, too, how many teachers have been so well drilled by fixed lecterns facing fixed rows of seats that they cannot emancipate themselves from spatial asymmetry when in the group room. They tend to take the biggest or most comfortable chair, placed at a greater distance from its neighbours than any of the others, at the head of the table if there is one, perhaps with books or notes in front of them, and in a hundred subtle ways emphasize the distinction between those who have come to teach and those who have come to learn. All this is done with the happy collusion of students; indeed, they may try to stop the teacher doing otherwise, for they also feel more comfortable in the familiar hierarchical situation.

A round table, if there is a table, and similar chairs, indicate that similarity of participation is expected . . . The furnishings of many classrooms resemble a court of justice rather than King Arthur's model of a round table for discussion among peers. In both, what is expected of the users is clearly defined by the seating accommodation. In the courtroom the judge, the juryman, the witness, the prisoner, each in his prescribed territory, behaves, while in occupation of it, in prescribed ways, the spatial relationships helping to denote his role, and supporting him in it (Hazard, 1962). By contrast, the round table denotes an absence of differentiation of roles; authority can flow around it from one mouth to another, and all are free to behave in all ways.

The importance of face-to-face contact in improving communication cannot be overestimated. Physical proximity is very important in human communication (Abercrombie, 1964; in this volume, see pp. 55–9) . . . In face-to-face contact control of intercourse by eye movements is possible (Argyle, 1967). For all our skill in telecommunications – phoning, or filming, or bouncing waves off satellites – it is still considered essential, when really important matters are under discussion, for heads of state actually to get together.

The geographical site is also important . . . The social climate that a group experiences will differ according to whether it meets in the teacher's room, or in its classroom, or in a borrowed room; and if it meets in the teacher's room, according to whether he makes himself wholly theirs, or fails to disconnect the telephone and disallow casual visitors. The social climate should symbolize complete dedication to the task; all associations to the topic of conversation will then be rightly regarded as relevant, and not to be dismissed as extraneous invasion, as the telephone or visitors would be.

These factors will be most powerful in the infancy of a group. Their influence wanes as the group matures, and it can be combated even from the start if members recognize it. The behaviour of the teacher, however, is a long-lasting influence on group behaviour; though the students' perceptions of it will change, they are always sensitive to it, and usefully so, because learning consists partly of internalizing the teacher's attitudes and values and ways of behaving. The teacher's role requires great self-discipline; he must get out of the habit of talking, and into the habit of listening. This is not easy, especially for teachers who have made a success of lecturing. Many who genuinely intend to encourage spontaneity and fluency of conversation among their students offer them a model which none should follow. They may be quite amazed to discover by listening to a tape recording or seeing a checked list of contributions, how little opportunity they have given anybody else to speak at all. [For further details and references, see Abercrombie and Terry, 1979.]

The expectations that the students bring to the group meeting will also affect their behaviour. Generally speaking, they will tend to expect the teacher to continue in the role of an authority figure to which they have been accustomed, and it is common for them to go through a phase of hostility and rejection when they find that this is not so. The more unfamiliar the objectives of the group work and its method of conduct, the more difficulty they will have in understanding them. It is therefore useful to state these as clearly as possible and also to have some record of the statement, written or taped. It is common for students when they have at last understood what it is all about, to expostulate: why didn't you tell us at the beginning? And for them to discover that in fact you had done so, but they had not taken it in, is quite a useful way for them to learn about the difficulties of learning. [For further details, see Abercrombie and Terry, 1979.]

Perhaps one of the nicest things about group work is that in our present state of ignorance students and teachers have to learn together, because the best way to learn about group work is to get on and do it. It becomes an absorbing occupation and, because one invests so much of one's personality in it, it is often frustrating and overtaxing. It is very important, therefore, to be able to share experiences with colleagues. Small conferences or workshops of teachers interested in group work which could meet for an intensive bout of discussion for a few days, or for briefer periods at regular intervals, could be very useful. They would help us to clarify our objectives, to describe our procedures with greater precision, to exchange and generate new ideas and, not least, to let us share our joys and sorrows.

King (1973), who questioned university teachers about their anxieties, says that in the seminar:

> Most had to do directly with the relationship with the students in what our respondents felt to be a relatively unpredictable and open-ended situation. How much freedom should be offered, either in expressing opinions or in the manner of expression? How could one maintain a balance between being too controlling and being too permissive? How was one to make sure that the time was used constructively?

Other anxieties concerned the organization of the seminar – how to draw all members of the group into the discussion, to elicit questions, to avoid silences, to make the seminar interesting without talking too much, to think of ideas 'off the cuff' if students were not responding, how to break down the initial silence, whether to wait for latecomers, and so on. Such problems occur over and over again in discussions when teachers get together to talk about their experiences of group teaching. Greater confidence in dealing with them can come from airing them in a supportive climate (Abercrombie and Terry, 1978a; in this volume, see pp. 153–60).

Group teaching and the objectives of university education

It remains to relate the aims of group teaching more definitely to the present educational scene and I shall attempt to do so for two of its aspects – the objectives of university teaching as described by teachers, and what students want.

The first SRHE Working Party monograph on teaching methods (Beard, Healey and Holloway, 1968) discusses the objectives of higher education from two standpoints. Beard, writing as a psychologist, elaborates on the systematic approach to the definition of objectives, including that of Bloom's *Taxonomy* (1954; 1956). Bloom considers objectives under two 'domains'. The cognitive domain includes objectives which run from the recall and recognition of knowledge, to the evaluation of information, or the making of judgements. In the other domain, the affective, the objectives range from awareness to the incorporation of beliefs, ideas and attitudes into a total philosophy or world view. Beard relates objectives to recent changes in higher education (for example, the introduction of greater flexibility in curricula and greater variety in methods of teaching) and to the psychology of learning. In discussing those processes which are largely unconscious, she says:

> In so far as more primitive learning processes are used, their function in higher education appears to be to foster confidence, to motivate students to learn, or to induce desirable professional attitudes; and since group influences are bound to operate, the composition of groups in teaching would be likely to repay study.

Healey and Holloway, in discussing the classical objectives of university teaching, concern themselves with the basic assumptions behind two main streams of thought, those of the liberal and utilitarian schools as exemplified by Newman and Huxley, respectively. Both regarded education as aiming to produce behavioural change in the learner, and the authors point out that, though not expert in the modern sense in pedagogical method, Newman and Huxley defined their objectives in a manner which is not too far removed from that of an educational psychologist today. The aim of the liberal school can be very briefly defined as 'the general awakening and training of the intellectual faculties and the provision of a broad-based culture', and that of the utilitarian school as 'studying and teaching those things which are useful to society as a whole'. It is, however, necessary to study the chapter carefully to appreciate the resemblances and differences between the two schools of thought in all their complexity and subtlety. One of the authors' thought-provoking statements is as follows:

> On the whole Newman's view seems to have held sway up to the present day in all *discussions* about university education, but it is the utilitarian one which has been used as a basis for *action*, both by successive governments and by academic planners, especially those in charge of the distribution of funds.

This brings us to the question of what students really want, for the disparity between theory and practice, objectives and achievements, may contribute to the present widespread dissatisfaction with university education . . . It is not so much that students have different objectives from those of the establishment, but rather that, as consumers, they have a clear perception of the ways in which achievement falls short of them. Most students accept the utilitarian and cognitive objectives. They know they need to learn in order to eat. Whether for their personal satisfaction, for professional gain, or to serve humanity, they need to become experts, to be able to master and manipulate a complex body of information within a specified area. But they hanker after the truly liberal education, the actuality, not only the promise or aspiration. Their motivation flags for learning what is offered in the curriculum; they feel their educators concern themselves less with the affective than with the cognitive domain.

A report by Blackburn (1968) of interviews with students of the University of Michigan, is relevant to the understanding of the behaviour of some of our students. Blackburn writes:

> The most striking aspect of these interviews is the extent to which they reveal how profoundly students are concerned with themselves, with their own personal and social development . . . If we turn from the almost completely personal to examine the influence of the academic environment on these young adults, the evidence is rudely disappointing. Their courses for the most part touch them only incidentally and apparently not by design. Portions of psychology courses occasionally reach a student and make lasting impressions, but the sciences and languages are at best tolerated and usually only by those who entered the University with a genuine desire to study them. They certainly attract no converts . . . Not only did students find the curriculum and the libraries remote to their concerns, they also recorded no meaningful contacts with the faculty.

He emphasizes the importance of peer relationships:

Their immediate peers, persons unknown to them a few months earlier, exert the most direct influence on them . . . contact with others in similar situations but from different backgrounds led them, as it does most students, to examine their own values, perhaps for the first time.

But while these peer relationships help Bloom's affective domain, it is clear they do not touch the cognitive objectives:

Although students are one another's most effective and impressive pedagogues, they teach one another almost nothing intellectual. They do not study together . . . They do not share ideas before writing a paper or undertaking a project. They do not critique one another's productions.

I hope it will be clear from the preceding discussion of varieties of group teaching that they can help to serve the various objectives of higher education . . . It is suggested that, if more learning were done in groups, the main objectives of both students and teachers could be brought closer together, the utilitarian with the liberal, and the cognitive with the affective.

The Distinctive Characteristics of 'Free' or 'Associative' Discussion Groups

From M.L. Johnson, 'Teaching by free group discussions', *Universities Quarterly*, 6, 3, 290–5, 1952.

The aim of free or analytical group discussions is to allow the subjective factors which influence the making of judgements to be exposed and recognized. The discussions are called 'free' because the students are encouraged to express themselves as freely and spontaneously as possible, and 'analytical' because an attempt is made in the group and by the group to trace the ramifying connections of the statements the participants make. We do not aim to get at the 'best' answer in the quickest possible time. Rather we try to identify gradually the subjective elements which have stood in the way of individuals getting a suitable answer.

The role played by the teacher in free group discussions is difficult to define. Of major importance is the establishing of a 'permissive' atmosphere. The conductor passes no judgements on a statement made, but only shows readiness to try to investigate its implications, in the course of which the extent to which it is right or wrong, useful or not useful, will become apparent. The tendency is thus to enquire into statements, rather than to accept or correct them. Perhaps the role of the conductor is best described as that of trying to set a pattern of behaviour which it would be useful for students to follow; the amount of self-discipline required by this will be apparent. The main component is listening attentively, a habit which it would be nice for doctors to have, but one probably not encouraged by the lecture system. It is necessary not only to listen, but also to show signs of having heard, and this is done by trying to work out the implications of what is said, to recall statements made in earlier discussions relevant to the present one, to show consistencies or incompatibilities in the reactions of different students, and of the same student at different times. In the early stages this gives the teacher quite a lot to do, but the students soon pick up the knack of doing it and take over themselves. It is then necessary for the conductor to say comparatively little – perhaps to supply factual information when necessary, to summarize the discussion at suitable intervals, or to show how, when it seems to get frustrated by detail, wider issues may be involved.

Comparison with other methods of teaching may help to make the essential nature of free group discussions clear. They differ fairly obviously from the lecture system in which . . . the emphasis is on the teacher *giving* information to the student. How what the student accepts differs *qualitatively* from what the teacher gives and from what the student does with it is not usually enquired into by either party. In free group discussions, the emphasis is not on giving information to the student, but on examining the ways in which information he already has is affecting, usefully and not usefully, consciously and not consciously, his approach to new problems and his reception of new information. Further, free group discussions stimulate the student to active participation, so that he learns by direct personal experience how reactions are subjectively coloured, rather than by report as he would in a lecture.

The differences between free group discussions and other kinds of discussion groups are not so obvious . . . I will attempt to distinguish free group discussions from the kind in which wide, controversial subjects are chosen as the topic. The main differences are: first, in the subject of discussion; second, in the mode of behaviour participants are encouraged to adopt; and third, in their main aims. First, in the controversial kind of discussion group, the subject chosen is one about which differences of opinion are to be expected; indeed, it would be disappointing and frustrating if none appeared. In our free group discussions (in medical education), on the other hand, the basis of discussion is the exercise, to which ideally the participants would react scientifically – that is, objectively, thus providing no differences of opinion. Second, as to mode of behaviour, in controversial discussions students are encouraged to defend and attack opinions and to stick to the point. In free group discussions, by contrast, students are encouraged to enquire into the validity and origins of the opinions expressed rather than to defend or refute them; they are not asked to keep to the point but to consider the possible relationships of apparently unrelated things, because it is only by following up an apparently irrelevant statement that its relevance for the student who made it can be unravelled. Third, the main aim of controversial discussion is presumably to help participants to decide whether the evidence presented makes one opinion more tenable than another – the emphasis is on argumentation. The main aim of free group discussion, on the other hand, is not to reach a decision on a debatable issue, but to expose to the student the extent to which his reaction to present stimuli is influenced by his past experiences, and thus to gain greater control over his behaviour.

Learning Processes in Group Analysis: Some Visual Analogues

From 'Foulkes and Escher: Visual analogues of some aspects of group analysis', *Group Analysis International Panel and Correspondence*, 1, 157–60, 1969.

That the present year (1968) celebrates the 70th birthdays of both S.H. Foulkes and M.C. Escher gives me an excuse to write about how the work of one, a group analyst, can be illustrated by that of the other, a graphic artist. An excuse seems necessary, because the connection which is so strong for me may be an entirely personal one, and may seem to other people to be no more meaningful than the coincidence that the two men were born in the same year, or that encounter with the work of either of them leaves one for ever after a different person. However, with or without excuse, an attempt will be made to describe some aspects of group analysis in terms of visual analogues, in the hope that this may help us to understand and master them better.

It is extraordinarily difficult to communicate, to one who has never been there, the subtle, rich and profound experiences of being in a group conducted by Dr Foulkes. Superficially the group has no obvious structure or palpable texture; it may seem formless, embedded in an intangible, floating vagueness. But Dr Foulkes's treatment of the group, or rather, one should say, his *participation in it*, is in fact highly disciplined, dictated by a sure perception of strong and rigorous, but changing, patterns of relationships. What may seem to the other group participants a serene, withdrawn passivity, is one manifestation of his intense involvement, and of his sensitive and steely mastery of technique. There is in Escher's art also, on first encounter, a deceptive simplicity, not mistiness in this case, on the contrary, an incisive clarity of representation which is both demanded, and made possible, by the very techniques he has chosen to command. But the patently precise relationships you first see turn out to be more and more complex, more and more ambiguous or polyvalent as you continue to look. The impact of some of his designs is similar to that of surrealism, and it is notable that one of the early ones demonstrates his interest in Bosch. But it is not a world of dream or of bogies that he mostly represents, of things being other than they are in real life – watches drooping or women sprouting trees – nor one of natural things in unnatural places, but rather it is the multiplicity of relationships between accurately represented things that he presents for us to discover. He is witty rather than sinister. Some of his patterns are endlessly repeatable and carry the imagination into infinite space, and others, however delimited as a recognizable unit, never let the eye rest with a global impression of the whole, but carry it dartingly hither and thither in all directions, as new relationships crystallize momentarily and as rapidly are replaced by others. Mathematicians and crystallographers have found his work relevant to theirs, as now I hope to show it relevant to some group analytic processes.

It is amusing to note that one of Escher's early woodcuts is of eight heads, four male and four female, forming an interlacing pattern, which recalls Dr Foulkes's preference for eight people, four of each, as the optimal number for group analytic psychotherapy. Another picture, a lithograph of startling and memorable beauty, seems to me to represent visually certain features of what Foulkes calls the 'group situation'. Its title is *Three Worlds* and it shows part of the surface of a woodland pond. The interface between air and water has fascinated other artists, notably Monet, but Escher's treatment of the theme is quite different from that of the great series of water lily murals. The water is unruffled, but dappled all over with a multitude of freshly fallen leaves, each as realistically rendered as for a botanical treatise. Three bare trees are reflected clearly in the surface of the pond and beneath it a huge deep-bellied fish moves sluggishly. His murky outline contrasts sharply with the stark reflections of the trees, which, although one knows they are superficial, can also seem to penetrate vertically down into the pond, because their shadows are interrupted by the leaves resting on the surface. The picture is quiet and contemplative, capturing a fragment of three worlds for a brief time within its own four edges, but spreading the vision and imagination beyond them. We do not know how far the pond extends to right or left, in front, or downwards, but the fish, the sort that is silently there one moment and gone the next, suggests that if a crust of bread were thrown on the surface, the shapes of many others would loom out of the unclear depths to join him. Each leaf is fresh from its tree, still dry and crisp, though one knows that soon it will get soggy, will be nibbled at by worms or grubs or bacteria and will slowly be absorbed into the pond, along with those that fell last year, and many a year before, its fragments dispersing in water and mud.

The group situation too is one of people sitting within four walls, but the walls only arbitrarily delimit it from other situations extending far beyond. The shadows of the world outside also belong to it. The members come together for a brief time; something new has happened, like, but also not like, many other events. The thoughts they express, each according to his kind, soon lose their discreteness and dissolve in the common experiences. Below the superficial social interchanges, powerful feelings stir in the deeper layers of consciousness, sometimes seen clearly, sometimes too dim to be properly apprehended, often invisible. They talk about the present in terms of the past, and what they do together affects their joint and separate futures.

The importance of being able to change the focus of attention rapidly from individual to group has often been stressed by Foulkes, and the alternation of perception of figure and background is an absorbing interest of Escher's. One of his designs is of light-coloured horsemen riding to the right, and their mirror images, dark ones, riding to the left. Their contours are common, so they completely fill the space, and each is either figure or background, according to the focus of attention. In a more complicated design the horsemen are pictured as though on a circular band of woven material, in which the figures which are light on one side show dark on the reverse side. Two edges of the band meet in the middle at the front, where two ranks of horsemen, four light ones marching to the right, four dark ones to the left, form a tightly interlocking group. Below this a row of light horsemen separate out and march to the right, turn upwards, and are seen on the inside of the band as dark horsemen marching to the left. As they turn downwards again they become dark, marching now to the right along the front of the band.

This treatment of the changes in appearance of an object according to changing point of view, or changing context, is marvellously developed further in other designs. A significant thing about Escher is that he does not disdain to write about his pictures in words; he struggles to communicate as clearly and comprehensively as possible, using whatever media. So I quote his words about a picture he calls *Day and Night*:

> Grey rectangular fields develop upwards into silhouettes of white and black birds; the black ones are flying towards the left, the white ones towards the right, in opposing formations. To the left of the picture the white birds flow together and merge to form a daylight sky and landscape. To the right the black birds melt together into night. The day and night landscapes are mirror images of each other, united by means of the grey fields out of which once again the birds emerge.
>
> (Escher, 1967)

Another woodcut is called *Sky and Water*. Black birds fly through a white sky above and white fishes swim in a black sea below. Where sky and sea join, the black birds and the white fishes are closely interlocked; their shapes are less detailed than those that emerge into the sky as black-feathered birds or those that sink into the water as white, finely-scaled fishes. These designs picture the closely interlocking relationships which are established in a group, and the way the participants draw apart, re-establish their own contours, and become individuals again as they leave it. Likewise they illustrate the emergence and clarification of thoughts, or attitudes, in the group process. In *Metamorphosis* a simple pattern of black and white gives rise to a continuous series of changing figures which arise from each other by association of ideas, just as in discussion in a group, ideas take form, become more complicated and then more simple again, evolving others in an everlasting series of transformations. A lithograph called *Liberation* deals with another aspect of metamorphosis. Escher (1967) writes of it:

> On the uniformly grey surface of a strip of paper that is being unrolled, a simultaneous development in form and contrast is taking place. Triangles, at first scarcely visible, change into more complicated figures, whilst the colour contrast between them increases. In the middle they are transformed into white and black birds, and from there fly off into the world as independent creatures. And so the strip of paper on which they were drawn disappears.

This seems to illustrate how in the very process of transforming, clarifying, identifying and emancipating, the group disappears, for the aim of group-analytic psychotherapy is to make the group redundant.

The rapid switching of viewpoint which is such an important feature of the group process is exploited by Escher in a series of prints dealing with spatial relationships. What is seen at one moment as the wall of a house may be the ceiling or the floor when seen from another viewpoint. To quote Escher (1967) again: 'The mental reversal, this inward or outward turning, this inversion of a shape, is the game that is played.'

Another most powerfully moving picture is that of a hand holding a spherical mirror. To quote Escher (1967):

> A reflecting globe rests in the artist's hand. In this mirror he can have a much more complete view of his surroundings than by direct observation, for nearly the whole of the area around him – four walls, the floor and ceiling of his room – are compressed, albeit distorted, within this little disc. His head, or to be more precise the point between his eyes, comes in the absolute centre. Whichever way he turns he remains at the centre. The ego is the unshakeable core of his world.

In the group one sees one's world in miniature, with oneself at its centre, but as the others talk, one sees *their* worlds, each with themselves as their centre, and with one's own world reflected in them too. And so, turn and turn about, one can see oneself from other angles; and get a more realistic view of the ego, even if it must remain the centre of one's world. Perhaps this is the core of the group process.

Neuropsychology and 'Associative' Group Discussion

From 'On evaluating preconceptions' in Tamil, P., Hofstein, A. and Ben-Peretz, M. (eds) *Preservice and Inservice Education of Science Teachers*, International Seminar, Jerusalem, Rehovot, Baban International Science Services, 101–4, 1983.

... My suggestion that some experience of associative discussion should be built into the education of teachers of science perhaps needs some further explanation. Its method involves introspection – the personal study of one's own mental processes, and its material is one's network of basic assumptions that profoundly influences the way each of us thinks, but of which we are for the most part unaware. It focuses on the inner world, increasing one's understanding of one's own by comparing and contrasting one's reactions to a given stimulus pattern with those of other people. Thus it runs counter to our currently preferred trend in education, concerned with educational technology, definable behaviourable objectives, and the notions of machine intelligence.

However, neuropsychology has recently taken a new turn in its study of the brain and consciousness, directing attention to the holistic practices of the so-called non-dominant hemisphere, compared with the analytic, sequential, logical ways of the dominant hemisphere. We need both of these styles of thought. The right and left hemispheres are linked with several commissures, the largest of which, the corpus callosum, is estimated to be made up of some 2000 million nerve fibres in man. Perhaps we could see associative group discussion as subserving in education the function of the corpus callosum?

Using 'Associative' Group Discussion to Improve Group Teaching in Higher Education

From M.L.J. Abercrombie and P.M. Terry, *Talking to Learn: improving teaching and learning in small groups,* London: Society for Research into Higher Education, 1978.

I was invited by the University Grants Committee to try to improve small-group teaching in universities. Three main approaches were adopted. First, weekly meetings were held of small groups of teachers, from different disciplines and institutions, discussing their current small-group teaching. Second, individual teachers and the students concerned had the opportunity to discuss with us video-recordings of their classes. Third, for large audiences, Paul Terry conducted discussions stimulated by the showing of excerpts from videotapes made from the first two approaches.

The groups were of between five and twelve teachers from a wide range of disciplines and from several institutions. One series of weekly meetings (64 in all) was run at University College, London. A total of 46 people were involved in these, some of whom attended on only one or two occasions, but 15 attended between eleven and sixty meetings. Other courses were of shorter duration (between three and sixteen meetings). In most of the meetings both authors were present as conductors, in some, one or the other of us.

The groups met in a small room, sitting in similar chairs around a small, low, circular table. Care was taken to avoid outside interruption – the telephone was switched off. The conductors were present when the members began to arrive and though the procedure was informal the meeting started and usually ended at the appointed time. Latecomers did not interrupt the discussion, but picked up the threads as it continued. Meetings lasted one and a half hours. There was thus a firm structure of time and place, within which the conversation could be relaxed and wide-ranging. It takes time for participants to get to know each other and for confidence to be established, so regular attendance for at least one term was encouraged; but members were free to join and leave as they wished. In the later meetings the presence of one or two seasoned participants naturally helped to set an effective climate more quickly.

It was not our custom to write notes during the group meetings, but to make a summary afterwards. A few group meetings were video-taped, and the discussions transcribed ... The meetings of one short-term group were audio-recorded and these also are reported ... In the latter case, the play-back and typed transcripts were used by the group. We have no doubt that the intensive study of its own development which recording makes possible could be helpful to a group which is sufficiently committed to take the time, but we have not fully explored this potential.

Discussion focused on first-hand experience of teaching in groups; this was the 'agenda', and within it conversation was more or less spontaneous. 'We're all battling up the same hill; we are coming to discuss it', one teacher said. The intention was to help participants to become better aware of what goes on in groups, and so to become more confident in handling their own classes. The aim was to bring the teacher's performance closer to his own ideal, which is often very high: 'I have a sort of image of myself being endlessly competent, endlessly capable, of giving superb tutorials and seminars, and setting up new teaching projects', said one, 'when in fact I'm scampering around for facts, not quite able to cope with what I'm doing already.'

In [what follows] we describe how we tried to establish a climate in which, by talking together, teachers could get a clearer understanding of their own behaviour in teaching and a stronger command over it.

[Chapter 7] The nature and nurture of group discussions

Four functions of group discussion can be differentiated which help to further the aim of helping participants to get better control of their behaviour in groups: the group can offer mutual support; can provide opportunities for increased awareness of one's own behaviour; can help to develop greater empathy with students; and can serve as a model for one kind of behaviour that can be developed in teaching groups. We will discuss these in turn.

The supportive nature of the group

As the teachers talk it soon becomes clear that no one's difficulties are peculiar to himself, and this is reassuring at the personal level. It also becomes clear that there are no trivial problems, but that all are related to very general and fundamental aspects of higher education which warrant intense and scholarly examination. This is reassuring at the professional level. The cumulative effect is described in a reply to the questionnaire (R51):

> I've seen big changes in other group members (of both long-term and short-term membership) – eyes opening to aspects of teaching that

previously were mysteries, new perceptions of themselves as teachers, deepening capacity to think out teaching problems. There's a relational dimension to this too, an increased mutual appreciation and respect as we watch one another change and develop in the professional context.

In addition to the generally supportive climate of the group, members often help each other to cope with specific difficulties. In some cases a teacher initially feels inhibited about introducing some situation which deeply troubles him. He tends to regard his problem as special to himself, particularly if the difficulties are of relationships with colleagues, or are closely involved with local institutional affairs. He does not believe they are worth talking about to outsiders who cannot (and maybe, in the interests of professional etiquette, should not) understand the intricacies of the multitude of personal and administrative factors that are involved. In such a case he may be reassured by another member who sees his own problem as basically similar. In one instance a member felt that unreasonable demands were being made upon him by colleagues, but was unable to protest. Another, from a quite different discipline and institution, described how he tacitly colluded with such demands:

> I think I can straight away see parallels in my own job . . . I feel my time is really being over-extended . . . I'm afraid to refuse because I don't want to admit my inadequacies, and, you know, you like to go on and on feeling endlessly useful to numbers of people.

They come to recognize that they are not being imposed upon so much by others as by themselves, in attempting to live up to their own image of the good teacher. As one said: 'It's much more of an internal thing, rushing around as an everlasting mother.'

Developing self-awareness

One person usually opens with a recent happening and others question and comment. It becomes clear that the incident described is only to be understood within a complicated situation – the relation of the particular class to the rest of the institution, the personalities of the participants (students and teachers alike), their past and current educational experiences, their immediate and more distant objectives.

As the teachers exchange ideas about quite small and concrete events, the networks of basic assumptions that we each have relative to education in general, and to the personal relations concerned in it, become manifest. Each of us is usually unaware of the assumptions which powerfully affect our own individual behaviour, and so we cannot question them. Faced with a wide range of alternative ideas, and a variety of modes of behaving to a specific event, we can recognize some parts of our idiosyncratic complex of assumptions and question their usefulness (for a more extended treatment of this, see Abercrombie, 1960). Statements taken from the questionnaires illustrate how some teachers have begun to recognize their own basic assumptions and question their usefulness:

> R55: At present I am aware of my own different feelings about group teaching – I 'grew up' feeling that individual tutorials were the ideal but now feel more enthusiastic about the possibilities in group work. The discovery that to develop new feelings about one's occupation is different from and more difficult than accepting new ideas, theories, about it, is going to be very important to me I know, and I feel a corresponding gratitude to those group meetings for this discovery. I suppose it is strange that someone engaged with literature, which demonstrates continually just that difference and relationship between ideas and feelings, should make the discovery relatively late; but then that very lateness confirms the difference between assenting to ideas and having an attitude from within one.

> R49: I know it's no longer so important to me to be constantly reassured that students like me. Nor for that matter is it so important for me to like them personally.

Talking in this way, participants learn to recognize needs which lie behind their motivations for teaching, and learn not to suppress these feelings, but to direct them into more effective channels.

It is important that the exponent is offered a number of alternative ways of behaving. It is not so much that his behaviour is criticized by participants, but that its implications, its possible effects on students, become clear and he is himself able to judge whether or not he should adopt a different approach. This kind of discussion is designed to help the participants to become more effective teachers, by being more sensitive to students' needs, better able to serve them and to command a range of roles. Examples of teachers' reactions are:

> R49: I now feel that I have a much greater range of different responses to group situations and therefore I find myself using this wider range, trying to find an aspect best suited to the needs of particular students in the light of my aims for a particular class or course.

> R45: I probably have less of a mania for 'coverage' since I have seen and discussed other teachers' methods of focusing on a single 'problem' in a seminar.

> R33: Previously I probably tended to tell students what I thought they should think. My first reaction to the discussions was the opposite – to try and be a permissive receiver of their ideas. I hope I have now developed some capacity for 'finding out where the students are and showing them how to take the next step'. I have also at the same time become aware that there are many emotional problems to be overcome in communication between students and staff.

Several respondents felt that their relationships with colleagues had also changed with their increase in self-awareness and confidence. Although the focus of attention in the meetings is on behaviour in teaching and learning, participants feel that wider areas of social interchange may also be affected. However, our aim is not to effect changes of such a generalized psycho-therapeutic kind, so the methods used differ from those of group psycho-therapy in general, and from allied techniques such as 'sensitivity training'. The conversation very rarely explores a person's distant past, as some therapeutic methods do, and is seldom concerned with current intra-group reactions. It seeks to illustrate the *effects* and not to unravel the *genesis* of habitual, idiosyncratic ways of thinking.

Some people do not find it easy to accept the implicit rules of these discussion groups. They find the conversation uncomfortably undisciplined or feel that it serves no more useful a function than casually 'talking shop' over coffee. A few are disappointed that we do not go further into psycho-therapy. But one wrote:

> I have learned to value highly the non-emotive atmosphere of the teachers' discussion group; through this I have been learning to be-have unemotionally in professional situations; or where some emotion seems desirable, I have the freedom to express as much as is desirable. The peaceful discussion of potentially intense situations seems to have given me greater control in work situations.

The maintenance of an effective social climate is of the greatest importance. The border between what can and what cannot be tolerated varies for different people within the same group, and for one individual from time to time, and the consensus within a group fluctuates. In time, the group becomes self-regulating . . .

Empathy with students

The teachers' experiences as a group of peers meeting with a conductor offer a model of some aspects of the groups they lead as teachers. An important function of the conductor is to help members to recognize how talking about their experiences may lead to better understanding not only of themselves, but also, through empathy, of their students. Thus in one group the conductor's (Paul Terry's) remark 'in a sense this was re-establishing a habit pattern that you have with students' was followed by Sam saying, 'What we're doing in relation to ourselves is something that we must be doing in relation to students too . . . We have certainly felt an inhibition about bringing in things which we thought might be taboo . . . but the students have felt an inhibition much more' . . .

A model for teaching groups

The teachers' group is not intended to provide a blueprint for members' own teaching groups; it could not do this because the content of discussion is quite different in nature. Its aim is to enable the members to prepare themselves to conduct the various kinds of class that are most effective for a range of objectives, according to need, circumstance and personal preference. By witnessing the behaviour of the other members of the group each person can recognize that a much wider range of actions is open to him than his present custom allows.

The conductor's withdrawal from the dominant teaching role, designed to encourage interaction among the other participants, illustrates to the teacher how he can liberate his own students. Perhaps the most significant thing to be learned from the conductor's behaviour is the habit of evoking conversation by saying little and listening a lot. As one of the participants commented:

> R49: Instead of viewing a group as an opportunity for students to understand clearly my thinking on some topic, I now regard group meetings as opportunities for students to clarify, communicate and to understand their own ideas about a topic. I am therefore much more silent in groups of students and try, with varying degrees of success, to behave less didactically than I used to.

The conductor's role

The method of conducting groups such as these has been developed over some thirty years since its basic characteristics were used in teaching medical students to behave 'scientifically' (Abercrombie, 1960; 1972). The present adaptation grew out of a brief experience of teaching Diploma of Education students at the University of Sydney (Abercrombie 1970; see, in this volume, pp. 82–3) and out of another experience of group work during a University Teaching Methods Unit course for teachers (Abercrombie *et al.*, 1972).

The conductor's task, directed towards serving the four functions outlined above, is that of encouraging participants to talk about their experiences of teaching, their overt reactions, and what feelings they have in relation to them, in such a way that each person can see more clearly what implications his behaviour has for the ways his students perceive and react in the group learning situation.

The conductor's aims and behaviour are thus different from those of the teacher with which we are familiar in the conventional teaching situation, whose main objective is transmission of information. In these groups, some teachers found this so contrary to their expectations that they were frustrated and disappointed and could not make use of us; others learned to tolerate and understand our behaviour. Some found the meetings of absorbing interest (not that there are no boring patches – even for the addicted). Individual variation in response to the same situation was marked. One teacher remained silent through a long stretch of a meeting because, as he said much later, he was intensely bored by assessment which was being discussed. Another was silent and withdrawn through the whole of one meeting because he was preoccupied with a crisis in his personal affairs which he felt he could not burden the group with. Perhaps the most obvious difference between the behaviour of a conductor and of a didactic teacher is to be seen in the amount of the class time he occupies in talking himself. It is this comparatively non-dominating behaviour that gives rise to the disappointment and even resentment that some teachers feel on first experiencing this method. It is this behaviour which the conscientiously syllabus-bound lecturer finds most difficult to adopt himself. Clearly the conductor talks less than a lecturer or seminar leader does, realizing that every moment he claims makes one less for the other participants to use. But he is not voiceless, for silence can be puzzling and even intimidating; participants must not be distracted from the job of struggling to express their own thoughts, and to understand others', by wondering, but not daring to ask, what an aloof conductor could possibly be thinking about. We do not want to give the impression that information or wisdom are being deliberately withheld; this would not set an example of the kind of behaviour we think useful in teaching groups.

In as many ways as possible the conductor behaves as other members do, as a participant-observer. As in all social encounters, much of his communication with the other members of the group is of a non-verbal kind. The conductor sits in the group, not apart from it. He cannot properly be described as 'passive', nor as 'silent except for summing up at the end', though some accounts of the method have described it in such terms.

It is important to learn to tolerate silences, and to differentiate between the different kinds; some are essential to allow for digestion, contemplation and reorientation, and can be quite prolonged; others denote embarrassment, disagreement or resentment. Usually it is helpful to enquire into these (though not always immediately); sometimes the cause is so well understood by all that comment is unnecessary. As far as possible, the conductor leaves it to other members of the group to manage silences, because a common mistake is for the teacher always to break them. However, the conductor may spontaneously, but sparingly, offer comments on his own personal experiences. This is specially important in the early stages of a group, as self-introduction.

Second to the need for self-denial in speaking is the need to devote oneself to listening, again a reversal of the teaching-by-lecture mode. The conductor listens hard, and tries to understand what each participant is trying to say and how this relates to the general stream of conversation. Patience is required, for the conversation is not that of scholars expounding their own subject – orderly, rational, polished, definitive – but rather that of venturers into unfamiliar territory. As Rachel said:

> I want to feel that if I'm going to discuss something I don't understand
> at all well, that I can stammer and probe blindly and so forth, and say
> silly things, just for the sake of starting to talk.

It is assumed that each member of the group has accepted the task of trying to improve his teaching in small groups, and that any topic that arises is relevant to this. The conductor has little need to act as a chairman who tries to keep the conversation 'to the point' – as he perceives it – because the aim is to investigate the points that concern members. So he helps to bring to light what particular relevance an apparent diversion has for its exponent and for the group (because it is unlikely that it concerns one person only). Modesty becomes a conductor – he cannot already know what is relevant to each person, but must explore jointly with the others, again a useful way for teachers to be able to behave in some circumstances. Stephen put it forcefully:

> Finding out with the students just exactly what the shape of our joint problem is. In fact there is a lot that we don't know about what each student's assumptions are about the material that he may be studying, and about what your assumptions are about each student, what he already knows, etc.

There are few conclusions or rounding-offs which may prohibit the re-opening of a subject; it is quite common for a theme to recur, either during the same session or in a subsequent one, as someone has second thoughts or finds himself able to formulate later what he could not say in the rush of conversation. A lot of work is done between sessions, recalling, rethinking, incorporating, associating with current teaching, so that a member may open one session with new thoughts on previous ones. Any member at any time may change the direction of discussion by bringing up an urgent problem, though some find it more difficult than others to 'claim air time'. The group learns to cope tolerantly with both greed and abstinence, as it permits recognition of its satiety with one person's loquacity and its curiosity to know what lies behind another's silence.

It is not strange that some people are uncomfortable in this discursive and sometimes seemingly chaotic discussion. For those who tolerate it, it is valuable because it permits the elucidation of the teachers' problems and helps them to perceive relevance in their own groups. Students tend to impose their own inhibitions on what they feel may be discussed in a class, even on a confession that they do not understand something. To quote from one group:

> Even not understanding the subject, however narrowly defined, is felt certainly by a lot of students not to be a legitimate thing to raise, or to be too dangerous to raise – they define themselves as stupid or something if they raise it.

The conductor helps to make the wide-ranging associative discussion acceptable by sanctioning it. He demonstrates its value by helping members to discover pattern and reason in each other's associations, even in apparently incidental behaviour such as the conversation of group members who have arrived early, or sub-groups which have formed before the group begins, group talk about the weather and group jokes. All these have significance in understanding the flow of group associations. However, the conductor must not appear to be omniscient, for as one teacher said:

> I think, probably, if you're going to try to establish some sort of discussion then the very last thing you want to do in your first seminar is to appear effortlessly knowledgeable, with all the answers just quivering at your finger tips.

The conductor refrains from dogmatic or authoritarian statements, and speaks tentatively, leaving openings for further discussion. He tries to set a pattern of enquiry and contemplation, rather than of criticism. He synthesizes and analyses, reflecting on the various implications of statements, trying to discern and make explicit the main themes underlying the various and sometimes seemingly unrelated contributions, bringing together things that are usefully seen as connected, and distinguishing between those that are better kept apart.

Above all, our aim is that teachers should appreciate their own abilities to learn by interaction with each other, so that they may continue to learn when the group has dissolved and are able to pass on this assurance to their students. Because they have successfully weaned themselves from dependence on a monolithic authority figure, they can better help their students to achieve one of the most important aims of education, to become autonomous learners.

Students' Attitudes to Professionalism, as Seen in Group Discussion

From M.L.J. Abercrombie and P.M. Terry, 'Students' attitudes to professionalism as seen in group discussion', *Universities Quarterly*, 27, 465–74, 1973.

Increasingly, in discussions on higher education references are being made to the need to make room for some kind of treatment of human relationships . . . Whatever ways are adopted, and a multiplicity of them is probably more efficacious than any single approach, they must somehow come to terms with the way the student is already thinking and feeling in relevant areas. A student on the verge of becoming professionally qualified, for instance, may already have quite strong feelings about the kind of social network he is about to enter. Whether or not the intention is to change them, he at least needs to become fully aware of them and of their implications for his interaction with others . . .

This paper presents a description of students' attitudes towards professionalism expressed during a series of group discussions which were part of a postgraduate Diploma in Architecture course. The course, which has been described in some detail (Abercrombie *et al.*, 1970) was oriented towards self-education. The aim of the discussions was to facilitate adjustment to taking responsibility for one's own learning, and for continuing to learn throughout one's professional life. Discussions occurred weekly over two terms, for a total of sixteen weeks, one group of students meeting with their studio teacher and the two authors in the morning, and the other in the afternoon of the same day.

Spontaneous references to professionalism were made sporadically throughout the series of discussions, but it is not surprising that as the approach of examinations became imminent, interest in qualifying intensified; the fifteenth meeting was devoted almost entirely to discussion of matters relating to professionalism. A general sense of disillusionment with professionals of any discipline was expressed . . . Professionals were seen as deceiving other people . . . Students felt that famous architects lacked the social concerns that preoccupied themselves. [The] fifteenth meeting . . . expresses the common preoccupations in different ways . . . In summary: in the morning session a student brought an article by the sociologist Paul

Goodman which he wanted to discuss; this seemed to summarize the main issues about professionalism which arose in the discussions and, in particular, which preoccupied these penultimate ones. The pace of discussion was lively; students made quick statements in quick succession; constant reference was made to external sources, citing various examples of professional behaviour from radio programmes, newspapers, the Goodman article, their own experiences in professional offices. In the afternoon the pace was much slower; there were long contemplative, ruminating passages concerned with somewhat irrational fears about assuming new roles. As conductors we tried to keep various ways of perceiving professionalism under consideration; in the morning we drew attention to the subjective 'inner conflicts' as we saw them, and in the afternoon to the more objective, realistic issues, referring, for example, to the different meanings that 'professionalism' might have. The discussion represents contributions from eight students, but from the nature of the discussions, and the content of earlier ones in the series, we see their statements as reflecting attitudes of many others in the class, in the school as a whole, and also in the wider national and international student scene.

The students associated with the notion of professionalism a rather confused web of ideas about elitism, specialism, expertise, bureaucracy and power. These associations are not adventurous... But it seems that our students were emphasizing only what they regarded as undesirable aspects of the characteristics that they discussed. The values they implicitly held would match those of the Royal Institute of British Architects (RIBA, 1969), that the function of the profession is to give an assurance of professional competence and integrity, that the architect is concerned to put his client's best interest first, and that he will do his work within the framework of a set of social and artistic values so as to ensure that the interests of society as well as those of his client are served by the best that architecture is able to create. But these students did not see the work of present architects as exemplifying these ideals.

What was outstanding throughout the series of discussions, covering over 50 hours, was the rarity of any statements of approval of professionalism. A sense of disillusionment, often very emotionally expressed, about architects, all kinds of experts, and powerful people generally, was paramount. They were described as being out of touch with reality, unable to see things as they really are, insensitive to the real needs of people and society and, therefore, unable to behave effectively. School principals did not see the curriculum as students experienced it; a general in Vietnam had acted in blindness and ignorance with disastrous results; the RIBA had arbitrarily made disadvantageous decisions about the future of some Schools; Corbusier had failed to interpret the needs of the people who were to live in Chandigarh. By contrast, students felt themselves to have a greater diversity of experience and therefore to be more aware, more in touch with reality, than their own parents or their teachers, or other members of the Establishment.

But worse still, the older generation, the authority figures, were not only ignorant, and insensitive, and ineffective, they also deceived: hollow men, they acted professionally, played a role, put up a false façade. 'Façadism' was discussed literally in architectural terms; examples were given of designers making the external appearance of buildings belie their inner structure. Professional behaviour was talked of in terms of acting a role, of donning frills, and discussion of a new design by a fashion expert for prison uniforms was elaborated into a hilarious joke.

The students seemed to be expressing a wide-ranging rejection of authorities. They selected from their experiences only such kinds of behaviour of authority figures as they interpreted as alienating. Almost the only occasion on which professionalism was seen as useful was where experts outwitted their colleagues for ends that the students approved. Examples were given . . . To these feelings of disparagement of, and alienation from, professional figures was added a fear of becoming like them. The discussions of the implications of becoming professional, of assuming new roles, included the expression of what might seem to be irrational apprehension. Students spoke as though they might lose their identity ('you don't know where yourself is any more'); or might become 'fragmented'.

There is nothing new or unexpected in the adverse reactions to authority figures which our students expressed. This is what the generation gap is all about, and it was particularly acute all over the world in this peak year, 1968, of student unrest. What we are here concerned with is the implications of such attitudes for higher education. Inevitably they bedevil a balanced and realistic consideration of the issues of becoming a professional. This involves not only becoming part of what Goodman describes as 'the hated system', but of doing so by acquiring skills from the experience of alienated, disparaged authorities. In spite of holding such attitudes students sit examinations qualifying them to enter the profession, and then work professionally in architectural offices. It was with the intention of giving an opportunity for such feelings and conflicts to be aired that the series of group discussions was offered, in the hope that students might begin to unravel the tangled web of denigratory ideas that they associate with professionalism. They might then more easily entertain the possibilities of becoming expert but not arrogant, specialist but not narrow, authoritative but not authoritarian, powerful but not insensitive; be able to perceive differences between people without feeling that communication was impossible; be able to make good use of other people's experiences even across the generation gap, and commit themselves to a professional way of life without losing their own ideas and their own identity.

Structure, Freedom and the Tutor's Needs in Group Teaching

From 'Overall review: the state of play', in Collier, K.G. (ed.)
*Management of Peer-group Learning: syndicate methods in higher
education.* London: Society for Research into Higher Education,
100–4, 1983.

The following themes (in syndicate work) can be identified. Perhaps most importantly, the need for a different attitude and way of behaving on the part of the teacher is clear . . . A second theme is the effect of the educational context on the conduct of syndicate work . . . It is interesting to note the acceptance of the idea that students (like children) when talking among themselves use a language which they can play with more comfortably and profitably than with that used by practised teachers. This supports the notion that the teacher's presence can actually act as a brake on students' mental development. Perhaps the most worrying and contentious theme is that of evaluation. Teachers are not only concerned with the technical difficulties of evaluating reliably and validly a method of teaching whose objectives are generalized, and aimed at preparation for a lifetime of continuing education. They are also concerned with the effect of examinations on the process itself, for example, the sensitivity of students to the changed perception of the tutor when, having relinquished the role of the authoritarian teacher, he takes on that of a necessarily authoritarian examiner. The solution of this dilemma is perhaps the greatest problem in the development of any attempt to encourage autonomy in students.

Structure and freedom

The special attraction that the syndicate method has for me relates to the way it makes a frontal attack on the problem of structure and freedom in higher education . . . Let us look a little closer at this business of structure and freedom, using a biological analogy. The human skeleton looks stable and durable in the museum – what more rigid and long-lasting? In life its job is to give support to soft flesh and blood and allow mobility of the whole body. It consists of separable rigid elements sweetly and smoothly jointed together in such ways as to permit sensitive muscles and nerves to perform their exquisite tasks. A man can do a range of movements that no other single species can command – he can walk, crawl, run, hop, climb, jump long or high, swing with a variety of strokes. Not only are the rigid bony elements so mobile on each other, but the architecture of each bit of bone is in life by no means static. Each is a whirlpool of metabolic activity, undergoing mineralization or demineralization according to stresses and strains of use, and the physiological state of the body; areas are eroded or extended by the work of regiments of cells that make or destroy them. In just the same way the skeletal structure provided for the syndicate, and necessary for its integrity, must be modifiable at anatomical and at molecular level, tingling with life, responsive to continual changes and extensions of demand . . .

There is one aspect of syndicate work which I think is not adequately treated [in Collier, 1983] – the teachers' needs (though these are certainly recognized). The adoption of behaviour which consistently and continuously encourages autonomy in pupils necessarily causes some strain in people who have not only been brought up, as most of us have been, in a culture thoroughly (though perhaps covertly) imbued with authoritarian attitudes, but who have made some kind of academic success in it. Self-selection plays its part in the recruitment of teachers; it is likely that those who opt for teaching are by nature concerned for the welfare of the young, and tend to collude with them in the authority-dependency relationship, feeling the need to be in control, looking after the fragile young with tender loving care. In syndicate work, they need to adapt to a divided role – one moment they are busy devising the essential academic framework; at another they spatially isolate themselves from the site of action; at still another they summon all to a plenary session, putting the final touches to the students' unfettered labours, adding, deleting, underlining, correcting. What a chameleon existence they must lead! Switching attention from an individual to a syndicate, or a group of syndicates; concerned with the body of knowledge, with facts that must be checked and rechecked, and with fancies that must be allowed to come and go; with skills social and intellectual; with likes and dislikes, loves and hates . . . Our own education, the tramlines of O and A levels, of degrees and diplomas, did not prepare us for this many-coloured task.

But even the most experienced could be happier and more effective if they had the continued support that can be given by the very same sources as provide the energy for syndicate work – discussion among peers. This also needs structure, but, academically, a minimum of it – a situation which gives people confidence to talk in a group, to find support in similarities of experience, and stimulation and enlightenment in their differences.

The Leader's Role in Small Discussion Groups

From 'Some notes on the leader's role in small discussion groups', *Contact*, 91, 1986.

Discussion groups can help people to be, and to feel, more effective. Most of us enjoy talking, and being listened to. Many attenders at large conferences express the view that the best part of them is the opportunity for random meeting and talk outside the formal sessions, over coffee or lunch. People are more likely to behave wisely and effectively if they have helped to make the decisions they have come together to discuss.

No two groups are the same, and the same group may be very different at different meetings. The degree of familiarity among members is an important factor. Members of a school staff group may know each other very well; teachers on a course may know each other only slightly, some groups are of complete strangers. Some groups meet only once or twice; some, such as working parties or committees, meet at intervals over some time. A group leader needs to be sensitive to the different requirements of a range of such groups.

The main job of the leader is to establish a climate in which all participants can listen and speak. The room should be quiet and comfortable (but not conducive to sleep) with similar chairs arranged in a circle, so that participants can see each other. Some feel happier with a table to put papers and their elbows on, but the boardroom look (long narrow rectangular table with a special high chair for the leader) should be avoided.

The leader must be wholly committed to the group and its works, never be late, or called away, or interrupted by his secretary or the telephone. He leads the group unobtrusively, largely by non-verbal means. He talks little, but his comments show that he has heard, considered and remembered what others have said.

He establishes and keeps the boundaries for the group, offering a clearly drawn structure for it, timewise. He starts on time, realizing that a person five minutes late who keeps the group waiting costs it five minutes per person – say 40 minutes. He acknowledges the late arrival by a nod or grin, but does not let him hold up his business. And he ends the group on time unless he has had its permission to carry on. He tries to keep to the agenda, or at least calls the group's attention to serious lapses from it. He warns the group when time is running out and helps it to rearrange the agenda if necessary.

Members should introduce themselves at the beginning of a new group, giving their name, job, and reasons for being there. Some shy people do not like doing this, but at least it allows them and others to hear their voice. Perhaps the leader should begin, in order to show the way, to set the pace and length of statement. I find that a group which is going to meet several times gets off to a good start if time is spent at first in paired interviews, one member then introducing his interviewee to the group. Some find it easier than introducing themselves at considerable length. The leader suggests they ask any questions that will give them information useful for working together – including why the interviewee came to the group, with what expectations, what he most looked forward to, and was most frightened of.

There are no fools in the group, and the leader shows no favouritism. Two kinds of participant may offer him special difficulties – the silent, and the over-talkative. Both of these can be controlled partially by non-verbal clues – the silent by perhaps an enquiringly raised eyebrow, indicating to him that the leader wants to know what he thinks. The over-talkative may quail if the leader fails to reward him by giving him signals of approval, by avoiding looking at him, nodding the head, and subsequently quoting him. If a silent person does speak he can be encouraged further perhaps by later reference to the substance of his remark, not necessarily giving his name. When there is a gap in conversation, the leader may suggest that anybody who has not had a chance to give their opinion can do so now.

The leader must learn to allow for different sorts of silence – the reflective, the anxious, embarrassed or puzzled. He should not be afraid of saying what he is feeling himself, and should not let silence stretch too long. He must be prepared to summarize discussion when useful, and ask if others' impressions agree with his opinion. He occasionally attempts to clarify discussion and compares and contrasts the positions stated by members of the group. He does not hesitate to express his bewilderment at times, knowing that others will share this.

At the end, he should recapitulate briefly what has happened in the session, note any decisions taken, and give the time and place of the next meeting and indicate the work to be done. He is the servant of the group and he will have served it well if people leave the session feeling satisfied with the work done, feeling supported and exhilarated by the group, and anticipating the next meeting with pleasure.

Part 4

Teaching in Groups: Examples of Practice

Preface

Part 4 contains detailed examples of courses designed and/or taught by Jane Abercrombie, using 'associative' group discussion as a central element. These are provided for three reasons: to demonstrate that the discussion and exposition of group teaching given in Part 3 grew out of professional practice and was enriched by it, that is to say, that there was a dynamic relationship between theory and practice; for the interest of teachers who wish to start or extend group work or to provide focus and structure for peer-supported learning; and to give some insight into her research methods.

All the extracts illustrate the principles upon which she based her educational practice. Every course in which she took a leading part involved face-to-face interaction among students, a changed role for the teacher, and recognition of the non-rational components of academic and professional education. Her aim was to help students to realize how and why they made intuitive judgements and to understand their own reasoning process, so that they could behave more effectively and with greater self-knowledge in their current learning and their future work.

I have not included, for reasons of space, extracts from any of her early educational papers (Johnson, 1942; 1948; Johnson and Bauer, 1946), though these show that she was experimenting, almost from the start of her professional life, with ways of training zoology students in scientific method, particularly observation, accurate recording, making rational inferences and arriving at sound generalizations; that her teaching methods at this time already included discussions with students about what they had seen and recorded; and that from early on she had begun to question what she called 'the crippling effect of too great a faith in authority' (Johnson, 1942: 58) on scientific progress. As she said in a retrospective paper: 'The quest began with a search for how to learn to see more clearly and comprehensively and make more reasonable deductions from what one sees' (1972: 124). These issues preoccupied her, throughout her long career as a teacher and group conductor.

However, it was not until the 1950s, after, as she herself testified, she 'had stumbled upon the work of Ames (1955) which so vividly demonstrates the influence of past experience on seeing, and had discovered the rapidly increasing volume of work on personality and perception' (1972: 125) that she began her pioneer course with medical students. This work also made her realize that

> the difficulties of behaving objectively, rationally and effectively in a wide variety of situations were connected with the perception the student had of his own relationship to knowledge through his relationship to knowledgeable people and therefore with his authority-dependency relationships ... The problem was how to take advantage of other people's experience without being confined by it, how to use old knowledge to behave effectively towards new and unexpected things' (1972: 125).

Yet, only the first two extracts in Part 4 are drawn from this important research, because a full account is available in *The Anatomy of Judgement* (1960; 1969; 1989).

Three extracts describe the two different architectural courses in which she was involved. These courses brought together in practical ways her interest in space perception, in the responsibility of professionals to be aware of and to respond to human need, in small-group discussion and in the problems caused for learners, especially in a time of change, by their reluctance to become autonomous. The one-year Diploma Course in particular added another dimension; it was designed not simply as professional education, but also as a piece of small-scale action research in which students, teachers and other participants continuously sought to monitor and improve the effectiveness and quality of the course. These extracts illustrate the difficulties and disappointments that students and teachers encountered; they report failures as well as successes.

Two extracts illustrate aspects of Jane Abercrombie's work with Paul Terry on small-group teaching for university tutors. The second of these is taken from the commentary which accompanied the videotapes (Abercrombie and Terry, 1974) which were made from their work by the University of London Teaching Methods Unit. Both papers give practical details (for example, numbers, seating and timing) and also summarize the main issues raised by the tutors as they considered, week by week, their own attempts to become more sensitive and skilled as teachers within small groups. Most frequently raised were problems of authority and control, the emotional aspects of teaching and learning, and the difficulty of knowing what pedagogical alternatives there were to didacticism.

Finally, there is a short extract from a paper written in the last year of her life which demonstrates the pedagogical versatility and flexibility of group-analytic methods. It describes one of a series of Cambridge Group

Work training courses for people working with small groups in a wide variety of occupations.

A further point needs to be made about the extract from 'A contribution to the psychology of designing' (Abercrombie, 1977a; see pp. 144–52). I have included this for two reasons. First, it gives detailed information about the content and conduct of small-group teaching. Second, I felt it necessary to include in the book at least one example of the transcript data which Jane Abercrombie frequently employed in her research, and to illustrate the use that she made of them. As is often the case in research which relies heavily upon quotations from tape-recorded speech, especially in groups, the argument advanced in this paper emerges rather slowly and sometimes appears to be obscured by the very data on which it is based. These are, however, problems of data analysis and use with which all qualitative research workers have to grapple. I make no apology for sharing them with readers.

Teaching Medical Students in Small Groups: General Principles

From 'Teaching in small groups', in Butcher, H. and Rudd, E. (eds) *Contemporary Problems in Higher Education.* London: McGraw-Hill, 119–132, 1972.

An account of the course of discussions that evolved over some ten years as part of a course for medical students has been published (Abercrombie, 1960). Its essential features can be outlined as follows.

(a) Attendance was voluntary. The course was not part of the examined curriculum. It was offered as an attempt to help to train students to behave scientifically, and was known to be part of a research project. The discussions were recorded for subsequent analysis, but students could at any time have the record deleted (they never asked for this to be done), and some use was made of extracts of the recordings to illustrate certain features during the teaching process. The research nature of the project had mixed effects on its reception. It tended to raise its prestige, but many students had difficulty in accepting that a project that was research-oriented could have a teaching value as well.

(b) The discussion sessions were firmly structured in time and space. There were eight sessions in the course, each lasting one and a half hours. These took place regularly in the same room and at the same time each week, and members of the same group of twelve people attended (although their attendance was voluntary, absence was rare). There were no casual interruptions, not even from the telephone. Participants sat in a rough circle, face to face.

(c) The ideological framework of the course was established by a demonstration of the basic principles of perception and communication. This showed how two people, or the same person at different times, looking at the same thing could see it differently. The factors affecting what was seen could be considered under two headings: the relevant experience of the observer; and the context in which the observations were made. Observer error in science was shown to be subject to the same laws as govern perception in ordinary life. The reception of information through the eyes was used to illustrate the processes involved in reception of information generally.

(d) Each session began with an exercise which was tackled individually.
. . . Comparison and contrast of their individual responses to these
exercises formed the basis of discussion. Each student was confronted
with various interpretations of the same stimulus pattern, made by
people like himself. He was not comparing his effort with the 'correct'
answer, as is usually the case, but was forced to consider his own and
other statements on their merits, and without the guidance and re-
striction of authority. It would appear, for instance, that what one
student took for granted as a 'fact', another regarded as an inference of
questionable validity, but then very soon, on another issue, the tables
would be turned.

By analysing the ideas that each student had associated with his
decision it was possible to tease out some of the factors that had caused
the differences between judgements. It was discovered that these factors ranged from minutiae of the immediate context (for example, the
precise typescript layout of a report of an experiment) to generalized
and deep-seated attitudes about human nature.

(e) The behaviour of the conductor was rigorously disciplined to serve the
aim of the discussions, to encourage each student to express freely his
personal reactions . . . In general, his aim was to make participants aware
of the tangled associations that existed between some of their ideas,
that might be better kept apart, and to see that some of those that were
rigidly separated might be better recognized as related.

Teaching Medical Students in Small Groups: Course Outline

From M.L. Johnson, 'A course on factors influencing scientific judgement', *Journal of Medical Education*, 30, 7, 381–91, 1955.

About six years ago, we set out to tackle some of the difficulties of medical education which cluster around what is often called 'learning to think' ... We took as our text a statement made by a committee of the Royal College of Physicians. The average medical graduate 'tends to lack curiosity and initiative; his powers of observation are relatively undeveloped; his ability to arrange and interpret facts is poor; he lacks precision in the use of words'.

Our aim to forestall these deficiencies ties the present course down to some of the everyday intellectual problems associated with the work of a student and future doctor. However much we may get tangled up with psychology or other recognized disciplines, we make no attempt at the systematic study of them. We try to get what Bertrand Russell has called 'emancipation from the tyranny of the here and now' by seeing how much our behaviour is controlled by factors which do not always help us to make the most useful response ... We hope that as we become aware of these determinants we can control them, thus making our judgements more 'objective' ...

The very freedom which is essential for the exploration of ideas is frightening to some people; a few feel that it is dangerous even to talk spontaneously. I think one of the most helpful things is to try to indicate the relation of apparently unrelated statements. The subjects referred to in discussion cover a wide range from Mendeleev's periodic table to the colour of buses, from Einstein's questioning of Newtonian physics to the effect of the London dock strike on the price of eggs. It is not surprising that a topic which seems vital to one participant is just a red herring to another until its significance to the main theme is pointed out. The aim is to try to replace the security of thinking in well-defined, familiar channels with a new kind of security based on the acceptance of ambiguity, uncertainty and open choice.

My role as a teacher in these classes is a rather peculiar one for I avoid telling the students what they ought to have done ... I regard my main job as establishing and maintaining 'free floating security' which helps students to adjust to this unfamiliar and often difficult situation.

Care is taken also to link up the discussions, and to show the series as an integrated one, despite the fact that there is considerable variety in the topics with which each discussion begins . . . In such ways deliberate efforts are made to make patent a useful pattern in what might otherwise seem meaningless chaos.

The outline of the course is as follows. The first three discussions are concerned with how we make judgements on information received visually.

1. **Observation: hand radiographs**. For individual work the students are given a print of two radiographs (of a child's hand and an adult's hand, respectively, although they are not told this) and asked to list the differences between the two hands . . . The selection of the kind of statements made appears in discussion to have been related to the student's interpretation of the question; there is disagreement as to whether inferences were or were not asked for. It is also related to the meaning the exercise has for the person; mostly, statements of fact are found boring and useless, while inferences are more 'important' or 'significant'. Only in discussion does it become clear that it is possible to make several incompatible inferences from the same data.

   Naturally the disclosure of the inadequacies of their personal approach to an orthodox exercise can be very disquieting to some students. I feel that it is important to show them that their behaviour is not extraordinary, but that generation after generation of students have made just those mistakes. This can be indicated by playing tape-recordings of extracts of previous discussions showing how other groups have fallen into similar errors.

2. **Observation: the rotating trapezoid** [in this volume, see pp. 36–7]. In this case the discussion is not preceded by an exercise but by a demonstration of the Ames rotating trapezoid and the aniseikonic spectacles . . . The impact of these demonstrations on some students is very powerful; one said 'But you can't have the whole world a jelly', and another 'It's as though my world was cracked open . . .'

3. **Observation: 'Seeing's Believing'**. At the end of the previous discussion the students are given a copy of an article, 'Seeing's Believing' (Johnson, 1953a), which discusses some general problems of perception and deals specifically with the hand radiograph exercise . . . The aim of these three discussions is to demonstrate some of the factors which influence the kind of information that is extracted from a specific visual experience. We hope that at the end participants will have absorbed some useful ideas on the role of interpretation in perception.

4. **Language**. Students are given a short quotation containing the terms 'average body,' 'average condition' and 'anatomical normal type'. They are asked to write what they think the author meant by those terms, and also to give all the definitions of 'normal' they can think of . . . During discussion the following points become clear. In some cases a person may think a word has only one, well-defined meaning. More often, people

think that a word is vague or has several meanings, yet in their reaction to the word, they may be very selective or specific. When a word has more than one meaning, the person using it partly prescribes its intended meaning by the context in which he uses it, but it may or may not convey the intended meaning to the hearer. When a word has several meanings, it may be difficult to keep them separate. There is little danger of confusion in cases where the different meanings apply to very different fields. When meanings are related and overlap, however, they tend to confuse thinking. Thus when the word 'normal' is used in an anatomical context (referring to the usual or commonly occurring), it is difficult not to be influenced in thinking by the physiological connotation of healthy.

5. **Classification**. The students are asked to write notes on this topic in preparation for discussion . . . In diagnosis we are using a classification system to help us to predict and to extrapolate. We use certain signs and symptoms as indications that the disease is of a certain kind or class – we give it a name. If we have correctly placed it in its class, we can predict a great deal more about the patient than we have been able to find out in the clinical examination. We exploit our own and other people's experience of similar cases. If we have placed the patient in the wrong class, our predictions will be wrong . . . Much of the information one gets from an object is dependent on one's assumptions about its nature, that is, about its appropriate class.

6. **Evidence**. Students are given a copy of a paper published in a scientific journal reporting some experiments and the conclusions drawn. They are asked to consider how far the conclusions were justified by the observations reported, and also to design an experiment to test the hypothesis which the author had tried to test. In assessing evidence, people are much affected by factors extraneous to the actual observations reported . . . [in this volume, see p. 17].

7. **Causation**. Students read part of a paper by Gregg (1949) which discusses the influence that the idea 'that each disease has its own specific, single and sufficient cause' has had on medicine. This exercise is clearly linked with the preceding one, for some problems of causation were already discussed there. It is also less specifically related to the whole course of discussions, for it opens with the statement that 'The past 75 years have been influenced by an idea so general and all-pervasive that it escaped explicit attention' and shows how an assumption can be both a good and bad influence . . .

8. **Summary**. In preparation for this last discussion students are asked to read a short article on group discussion (Johnson, 1953b). We attempt to review the course, discuss its aims and techniques, and what the students feel are its effects.

Summary

... It is fairly well accepted now that it is useful to study 'what kind of fella's got a bug' as well as 'what kind of bug's got a fella'. Soon perhaps it may be more widely accepted that it might be useful to study what kind of student takes a curriculum and how he reacts to it, as well as what kind of curriculum a student takes. For it is not unlikely that the capacity of a medical graduate to be curious and full of initiative, to observe accurately and comprehensively, to arrange and interpret facts wisely, and to use words with conscious precision, is related to what kind of adjustments he had to make as a student to the impact of his medical course ...

Understanding Human Behaviour: Teaching Psychology to Architecture Students

From 'Psychology and the student', *The American Institute of Architects Journal*, 48, 3, 89–92, 1967.

The need for architects to have some understanding of human behaviour is now well recognized. However, psychology is as prolific as any subject that has contributed to the information explosion. The problem is one of selection. Of all the information in psychology that is available, what are the essentials for an architectural student, keeping in mind that he also has to learn about the more technical aspects of designing the built environment and that these too have multiplied prolifically?

At the Bartlett School of Architecture, we made three decisions about the teaching of psychology. First, we decided to focus on two main areas of behaviour: space perception and small-group behaviour. I hardly need to spell out the importance of both of these for architects, but I do sometimes feel uneasy about our choice, because these two areas happen to be those I was most interested in before I came into architectural education. There may be others just as crucially important to architects.

The second decision was that we should not treat these subjects in the accepted academic way, as though for psychology students, but should integrate them thoroughly with the main job of learning to design, hoping to avoid the well-known difficulties of transfer of training.

Third, we decided to treat the subjects in a personal way, making deliberate attempts to help the individual become aware of how his habits of thinking and doing, his unconscious attitudes and assumptions, affect his behaviour in matters relating to architecture and in learning to become an architect. The hope was that this insight into the factors that affect his own behaviour would help him to work more effectively . . .

Space perception

In deciding what we expect students to learn, we rely heavily on American work, especially that of the Ames School (Ittleson, 1952), the Gibsons

(Gibson, 1950; Gibson and Walk, 1960) and Sommer (1959) [see also Sommer, 1969]. We emphasize the importance of bodily movement for the perception of architectural space. This tends to get neglected if teaching is based on what is so important for painters, that is, the veridical representation of three-dimensional space in two dimensions, as seen from a fixed viewpoint. We emphasize the importance of social space, of the perception of personal proximity and distance. We emphasize the symbolic significance of spatial relationships . . .

We remind students of the way people behave in response to their perceptions of space, whenever their design would improve if they took note of it. Thus, when designing a school for young children, the students will consider questions of siting, distance from home and the placing of cloakrooms and toilets, with reference to the infant's need for a sense of proximity to its mother . . . In designing the classrooms, they will recall what they have learned about the symbolic meaning of a teacher's mobility in the classroom, contrasting this with the symbolic meaning of the rigid layout and fixed furniture arrangements of courts of justice (Hazard, 1962).

This kind of information will be recalled again when the student is designing an outpatients' department of a hospital; and, when designing a residential centre for management studies in the country, he will recognize how the users' perceptions of the relations between town and country, home and away-from-home, will form the background to their studies, profoundly affecting how and what they learn about the management of men.

As to the personal message of all this to the student – how it will alert him to his own space perceptions, helping him to use and enlarge upon his own spatial experience – this we hope to facilitate by our choice of the time at which he will receive this information. It occurs during his first term . . . Often this is his first experience of being separated from his family for any length of time by physical distance. Almost invariably, even if he continues to live at home, he becomes separated from it by experiential distance; indeed, the very thing he came to the university for will not be achieved otherwise.

In order to help the student come to terms with this experience and relate it to the job of being an architect, his first project is called 'Living in London'. In recording his experiences with sketches or photographs, he applies what he has learned about the representation of three dimensions in two dimensions – of overlap, linear, textural and aerial perspective, and so on. He is also encouraged, by discussion and reporting, to become more conscious of his own reactions to the spaces of his bedsitter and studio, of streets, squares, tunnels and towers, in a way which helps him to understand how the behaviour of people in their millions is influenced by the subtle and complex impact of the man-made environment.

We encourage the development of sensitivity to comings and goings, entrances and exits. In their second term, the first-year students are asked to help with our selection procedure by looking after the candidates who come up for interviews . . . They are asked to remember their own reactions when they went through the ordeal a year earlier. In the second year, a project on a health centre brings up again the question of entrances. Should there be separate doors for patients and staff? Around this problem feelings arise about status and role differences, and the wish for, or avoidance of, familiarity between authority figures and dependents. The efficacy of a doctor (and of a teacher) who dispenses with the institutionalized symbols of a role are debated. We are soon discussing new orientations in medical care and education, away from the notion that medicine in a bottle is all a patient needs to cure his ills, or information in a textbook all a student needs to cure his ignorance.

In the fourth year, exits and entrances come up in relation to the students' reactions to pain, disease, chronic sickness or accident. They design an outpatients' clinic, and the specific question raised is: should there be a single large waiting room for patients and their friends from which the patients alone would be filtered off to the various speciality clinics, or should there be provision for the patient's friends to accompany him to the speciality clinic, each of which would have a small waiting room for this purpose? One student scoffed at the notion that people might be frightened of going to a hospital. He agreed that a child might, but not an adult; he would not, of course, be frightened himself. But he could see the point when another student said that he had not been able to remember what the doctor had said to him, and others recalled having been confused at an interview and unable even to listen to what was said. It was agreed that, whether or not a patient needed emotional support, it might be better for a friend to remain with him for as long as possible, simply in order to facilitate communication. The doctor might find it a help, too, to have a quick and easy access to a less confused source of information than the patient himself.

This sporadic recalling of relevant psychological principles is facilitated by my being around in the studio at key times, as when the studio teachers are introducing a programme. I want to emphasize that this sort of learning is economical of students' time. It results from taking action in the studio and not from grinding away at a textbook of psychology. Time and place are important for the making of associations; children tend to classify objects by spatial and temporal contiguity before they can handle concepts and generalizations. As adults, we all have remnants of such primitive ways of behaving, and we might as well get them to work in our favour rather than against us.

Along with this teaching, we are exploring the relation of spatial abilities, as measured in psychological tests, to the design process. As part of our research programme, students take several tests of spatial ability. These are discussed with them afterwards so that they can learn how psychologists analyse these aspects of mental function in, for example, the possible disadvantageous effects of school examinations, which are of a verbal-intelligence nature, on the recruitment of students to science and technology.

I would not suggest using tests of spatial ability to eliminate students but rather to help those we already have. It may be possible to improve studio training by introducing specific exercises based on some kinds of behaviour tapped by such tests . . . In their first year, students may not have fully developed their powers of spatial visualization due to lack of experience. We hope to quicken this learning by designing exercises for this purpose and by making students aware of the intellectual processes involved.

Group behaviour

As with space perception our students are given relatively little content in their study of group behaviour. (An indication of the area covered is given in Abercrombie, 1960; 1965.) The study of the two areas is very closely linked . . . Integration with studio work, since spaces are designed for various groupings of people, is fairly straightforward.

It is in the field of personal development that knowledge about group behaviour, and experience of it, are most intensively used . . . We introduce various kinds of group work into the course which act as models of the kinds of work situation the young architect will meet. They also help him to develop a more general self-awareness and skill in dealing with human relationships.

We experiment with different kinds of group – different sizes, some self-selected, some staff-selected, some for information seeking, some for designing . . . The most ambitious piece of group teaching that we have undertaken so far was with a fifth-year class of thirteen students, half of whom had been in the school for four years. The others had joined us a year before, having taken their first degree at another school, which had a differently oriented course. It had been decided that in the final year the class should be given experience of tackling a planning problem that was of such a size and complexity that an individual approach would be inadequate – a team was necessary. This work was to take place in the spring and summer terms. Two kinds of working experience with other people were planned in preparation for this team work.

During the autumn term, the students worked individually, designing a school which was to be built with an industrialized system, and for this they made use of experts, as they would need to do in practice. On Monday afternoons the class met with three experts (a quantity surveyor, a structural engineer and a services engineer) who ordinarily function as members of a design team. The class met beforehand to discuss the questions which they would put to the experts. The emphasis was on information seeking. Although difficulties of interpersonal relations would undoubtedly impede the communication process, as in real life, they were not discussed at these meetings any more than they would be in real life. On Thursday afternoons, meetings of quite a different kind took place. The class met with me and one or two tutors for informal discussion, to explore the design process and the difficulties which interpersonal reactions might put in the way – both of each person working individually and of a group attempting to work together. This series of meetings was introduced with some general principles of group behaviour, that is, the supportive nature of groups based on early mother–child and family relationships, the tendency for supportive groups to become exclusive (this had special relevance to the dual origin of this group), conformity in groups, non-conformity as in synectic-type groups or true teams, and group experience for encouraging a flexible attitude. The class saw and discussed *Twelve Angry Men*, a film about a jury discussing a murder. It was shown to the whole school as an introduction to group behaviour and discussed in 'vertical' groups, that is, groups containing students from each year. This was an appropriate and productive occasion for the different ages to mix on an equal footing, for the film clearly brings out how each individual interprets evidence differently according to his basic assumptions about human nature. It raises problems of leadership, and how the role of the leader (if there is one) and of the participants can be varied effectively to meet the aims of a group. We discussed also a group project that the class had engaged in during the previous year (designing an exhibition) which had failed because of interpersonal differences, and we examined the reasons for this failure.

The project for the spring and summer terms was the design of a new town. The students were divided into four groups. We took some trouble to make each group as balanced as possible, taking into account the strengths and weaknesses of the students in analysis and design, their backgrounds, personalities and attitudes. The groups were not self-selected, as student groups are. Instead they resembled professional groups. It was made clear to the students that the aim of this experience was to teach them to design for team working. It was not expected that the resulting designs of the town would be as good as might have been achieved if the students had worked in self-selected groups (although as it turned out, the designs were, in fact, very good).

The idea was to use the design project as a vehicle for learning to work in teams. Some of the stumbling blocks to this which had to be overcome were very common habits, such as unpunctuality. One team broke down because half of it preferred working in the early part of the day, and the other half in the later part . . . The students' reactions to this group work were, as one might expect, various and variable. Although some were puzzled and frustrated by the unconventional and self-conscious set up, several of them have since said that they learned a great deal about group work. One student, towards the end of the period, said that for the first time in his life he had not felt possessive about an idea. Another said he had learned to listen, and another realized that other people can have very good ideas – if one can learn to understand them.

The students whose education we are planning now will not even begin to practise until five years have passed; they can expect to be still at work in 40 years' time. As to the kinds of work they will be doing, their aspirations, their techniques, the environment that will affect them and that they will influence, the only thing that we can say about these is that they will be different from ours. We are therefore trying to educate for change, to help our students to learn how to learn. We believe that this can be done by the application of psychology to their education in such a way that each can learn not only about how other people behave, but also about the factors that affect his own individual behaviour, so that he can get better control over those factors and thus do more effectively what he chooses to do.

Using Action Research in the Design and Evaluation of a Course for Architecture Students

From M.L.J. Abercrombie, A.J. Forrest and P.M. Terry, 'Diploma project 1968–69', *Architectural Research and Training*, 1, 6–12, 1970.

This paper is offered as a contribution to the literature on action research on architectural education – that is, it reports a specific example of the introduction of planned change and observation of its results . . . Our project was located in a small site (a one-year course in a particular school of architecture). It involved a great deal of participant observation, not only by the researchers but also by the other participants in their various educational roles . . . Its 'primary diffusion channel' was continual feedback to the class itself. It may be appropriate to use [*Architectural Research and Training*] as a 'secondary diffusion channel' for wider dissemination of its results, because many other schools are experimenting on similar lines . . . The responsibility for writing this report has been taken by three of us, and we are well aware that it gives only a very fragmentary picture of what happened. It is quite impossible to represent at all accurately and comprehensively what any one of us felt, let alone do justice to what all of us experienced. The need to condense and make explicit gives the impression that the project went more smoothly and rationally than it did. It was, as one student described it, a messy operation; we were groping in the dark, often confused and frustrated, sometimes apathetic, stubborn, stupid and angry.

Objectives

The initiation of a new one-year Diploma Course in 1968 gave us the incentive and opportunity to intensify the Bartlett's efforts to lay some firm foundations of general education as a basis for the development of professional effectiveness. Very generally, we may describe our aims as those of encouraging students to be sensitive to the human needs that are satisfied by the characteristics of the built environment; to be strongly motivated to satisfy those needs; and to be equipped to do so effectively. By 'equipped' we mean, at the minimum, having the necessary professional qualifications

– but if these are to be used effectively, certain attitudes or ways of behaving are also necessary. For instance, one needs to be perceptive, adaptable, resourceful, responsible, and mature. One needs to learn how to continue to learn, in order to cope with changes in future professional demands. One needs to be equipped to take charge of one's continuing education, and for this one has to emancipate oneself from dependence on teachers. More specifically, four main objectives of the Diploma Course could be defined: to encourage education for change; to improve skills in advanced architectural design; to develop effective attitudes to the professional role; and to prepare for team work in professional practice.

Methods

In the initial planning of the course, certain decisions were taken about its structure and content which attempted to establish an educational climate that would be conducive to achieving these objectives.

Of the students – 25 altogether – a third had come into the Diploma Course directly from the third year at the Bartlett; a third after a year in practice; and a third from other schools of architecture (Berkeley, Cambridge, Colombo, Copenhagen, Hammersmith London, Newcastle, and Troy USA). We hoped to take advantage of this variety of experience. A full-time member of staff would act as year coordinator and three other full-time studio tutors would participate for one term each. Two members (not architects) of the school's Architectural Education Research Unit (AERU) would work closely with the project throughout.

The intention was to give students much more responsibility than hitherto for their own education by involving them in planning the course, choosing their design projects, and assessing their work. This was in line with trends in some other schools of architecture and, of course, with the requests or demands for profound changes in educational climate which were being made by many students and teachers all over the world. The role of the studio teachers, for instance, was intended to be participant rather than didactic or authoritarian. The class was to be divided into two parts, each with a studio tutor who would have a particularly close liaison with his group and would contribute to its experience and ideas at all stages of the work. Professional consultants (quantity surveyor, structural engineer, mechanical engineer, building technologist, town planner, sociologist and systems analyst) were to be available to the students at their own request.

Particular emphasis was to be put on the importance of gaining experience of collaborating with various people and various sizes of group, in order to prepare for team work in practice. The two parts of the class allocated to a studio tutor were to be so constituted that they consisted of a mixture of students of the three different origins, bringing variety of experience to the group.

The content of the course was planned as follows . . . It would provide opportunity for 'free group discussion' at weekly meetings of each half of the class with its studio tutor, conducted by the two AERU members (see Abercrombie, 1960). The aim of these discussions was to improve effectiveness of behaviour by making apparent the kinds of factor which in ordinary circumstances influence a person's behaviour without his being aware of them ... The course of 'free group discussions' was to be introduced by a lecture-demonstration, and reading material was to be given on elementary principles of relevant aspects of psychology (perception, communication, construction and human relations). In order that these general psychological principles might be usefully applied to the specific needs of the architect in training, references to problems arising in the current studio projects were to be encouraged throughout the discussions.

As to assessment, we recognized that this is an extremely important factor in the educational environment. It was intended that mutual and self-assessment should be encouraged as part of the education process, at the same time remembering it was necessary to satisfy the examiners that the year's work would exempt students from the Royal Institute of British Architects (RIBA) Part II examination ... The University College regulations required at least one formal written examination to be held toward the end of the academic year.

Finally, the stage was set from the beginning for observation and research as well as for innovation. Participants agreed to become involved in the AERU's research project on attitude change. For instance, they responded to a series of complex and demanding tests for measuring attitude development and agreed that the 'free group discussions', which were intended to catalyse the educational processes, might be recorded for analysis. It was planned to feed back results of this research as they became available.

It has been necessary to explain these intentions in some detail in order to make the consequent changes in emphasis more meaningful. Up to this stage the planning had been done by the staff. This was necessary, but contradicted the ideas about participation which they were putting forward. However, the plans were presented tentatively, so that the students could make changes they found appropriate to their own needs. Most of the first week was spent discussing the plans.

Results: Response and evaluation

In attempting to evaluate the extent to which we succeeded in our aims, we called on three sources of evidence. The first of these was a quite conventional one: the observations the studio staff made, in daily contact with students, of their method of work, or of their design products as presented at reviews, or of written reports. The second, less common in architectural schools, was provided by students' self-observations. At the end of the second term the students were asked to prepare dossiers (diaries or logs, comments, and so on) of their activities throughout the course as a complement to the conventional evidence of design studies they would be handing in at the end of the year. The third source of evidence was still less conventional than the students' written words; it was their spoken ones in the 'free group discussions'.

Observations of studio staff

Before the beginning of the session, a paper was distributed which outlined educational methods which it was hoped would be incorporated into the Diploma Course. This was to serve as the basis for establishing the direction of the year's experience: that the students and staff together should plan and manage the curriculum. The students showed an immediate enthusiasm for the outlined proposals and in the first three weeks completed designs for a closed brief. They then formed, apparently on the basis of social and intellectual compatibility, self-selected work groups (mostly of four people, but one man worked alone) for their 'open' studies. As they worked on these, they tended to arrange events (such as visits to old people's day centres or to a tower block in the area) in a rather spontaneous, impulsive way, and they were not able to cover the range of problems as they might have done with more systematic planning. They generally concentrated either on broad socio-political-economic issues or on excessively narrow ones.

The second term began with widespread frustration and lack of confidence in developing further studies. Self-selected groups formed with considerable splitting and reshuffling of the previous groups. Some who had felt most incapacitated in their initial group or had worked alone, tended to form small new groups, often pairs. Some of the more successful big groups split up partially and worked more in pairs or individually (for example, on quite different design schemes sharing a common site). As the term progressed there was less and less participation as a community (most groups worked at home), little contact was sought with the studio staff in formulating work programmes, and little use was made of the consultants. Above all, there seemed a great reluctance to participate as a community in mutual assessment.

We had all been troubled by the problems of assessment from the very beginning of the course. Students had expressed much concern, particularly when they met with the external examiners, about how their learning in this relatively free context could be assessed. The external examiners recognized their responsibility to the college and to the RIBA, but without specifying rigid or exclusive requirements. Nevertheless, a dilemma was posed for all, and the students tended to withdraw more and more from any form of assessment, by each other or by the examiners, and sought out studio staff only to make personal comments on their work ... The outstanding exception (to this self-imposed isolation) was that of the largest and most cohesive group of six people, who had worked together day and night preparing their presentation and had invited other members of the school to see it . . . They presented quite radical design philosophies, in conjunction with varying kinds and qualities of design products . . .

Some students reacted less dramatically than this to the open brief by choosing specific, well-established types of building (for example, schools, swimming pools), stipulating certain constraints but also including some of their personal values (such as raising the standards of the environment, increasing spatial flexibility). In effect, at one extreme there was a tendency to expand the professional role quite outside the domain of architectural expertise (for example, into political activism), and at the other to accept the existing architectural constraints and subtly incorporate some personal values . . .

While continuing to work on their designs, a number of students came together to work on plans for the MSc course which they might take after the diploma year. Critical of the structure and content of the projected course, they collected information from other members of the school and succeeded in bringing about constructive changes in the plans . . .

By contrast, the case studies inspired little enthusiasm. The first of these was the study of a school which two of the studio staff had designed and which was near completion. It was planned that the students in the groups should interview the architects, as though on behalf of the client, and study tape-recordings of the transactions to improve their techniques of collecting and reporting information. There was little student involvement with this staff-organized task. Subsequently students chose their own case studies, and some of these were pursued with vigour, but there was little interaction around them . . . In the final term there was a general tendency to break away from group work and pursue individual projects and prepare for the examination . . .

Throughout the course there was a growing concern about professional integrity . . . [See Abercrombie and Terry, 1973; in this volume, pp. 112–14.]

Students' observations

The suggestion that dossiers should be prepared resulted from the recognition that many of the students had chosen to work quite independently, and the staff might have little knowledge of their activities . . . The request also took account of the fact that the course was a more inclusive and subtle learning experience than could be assessed by the usual submission of design products . . . Consistent with the policy of the year, the students were free to develop their dossiers on the basis of their personal experiences. Specific observations were the more significant because they had been determined by the students' own selection from the year's experience.

Not surprisingly, the articulation of the year's experience was very difficult, especially for people whose main medium of expression was non-verbal. Not only had it been a powerful and very mixed experience, but several felt they would understand it sufficiently to write coherently about it only after a lapse of time . . .

Education for change

Throughout the reports there was a very strong feeling of optimism about the year's experience, connected with a new sense of confidence as self-educators and designers . . . Difficulties were recognized also: references were often made to the 'turmoil', 'distress' and 'uncertainty' experienced during the year because it represented, as one student explained: 'An effort to let the design conflicts come to a head and to discover the reasons behind them. For the first time I felt that I was left with a fundamental integrity that I could distinguish as being my own and which I could use as a sound basis for designing.' . . .

Professionalism

Increased awareness of professionalism was reported as coming directly from the new educational experience: (for example) 'I think the course has been professionally oriented, making students more aware of their education, evaluating their self-education and trying to define their role in society'.

There was in general a concern for professional involvement with wider issues than hitherto considered . . . There were doubts about the breadth of concerns that could be tackled: 'Whether we architects could solve the problems of a community which is more social and economic than architectural . . . I am not sure – but that is one of the experiences gained.' At the same time, there was concern for direct, personal professional interaction, with special emphasis on the ability to communicate professionally in more flexible ways . . .

Team work

A wide spectrum of group activities was reported . . . Along with this diversity of group experience there was an appreciation of many of the problems in groups – for example: the appropriate life-span of a group (for example, 'The group had outlived its usefulness, so it was disbanded'); the need for a shared group vocabulary ('An important discovery, at least for me, was the need to understand architectural concepts, a common conceptual framework, so that we could begin to understand each other before we had become bogged down in differences of opinions that were in many cases illusory'); the ways of working as individuals within a group ('I used the group to develop my own ways of thinking. For example, I helped to establish a group policy and then would become a critic of it, which inevitably sparked off some very productive discussions'; 'We worked out our individual philosophical positions within the context of a group's testing bed') . . . Finally, reference was often made to the importance of the variety of group interactions . . .

Observations from the free group discussions

These discussions were introduced by a lecture demonstration which was important in establishing the quality of the group experience that the course was to provide: that is, the lecture was not of the traditional information-giving variety, but instead it questioned unrecognized assumptions about perception and communication. Reading matter, intended to provide a firmer, more theoretical basis for this view, was issued so that students could make use of it, how and when they pleased. Consistent both with the policy of freedom for the year and the basic principles of the 'free group discussion' method (Abercrombie, 1960), no closed, fixed solutions were proposed; the lecture was offered as a provocative introduction to a free group discussion experience.

Participants, both students and staff, took this freedom even further than the group conductors had anticipated. They chose to scrap the formal subject matter and only fleetingly referred to the literature which had been supplied; instead, they used the discussions to further their understanding of the new learning experience. This was not altogether surprising ... we were experiencing, many of us for the first time, the problems of redistributing power and responsibility between students and staff. Both found the desired changes difficult, sometimes painfully so.

The discussions involved very subtle and complex exploration of attitudes [see Abercrombie and Terry, 1978b]. These are here discussed in relation to the four objectives mentioned earlier.

Education for change

The freedom and openness of the structure of these seminars made them in many ways a microcosm of the year's experience. Throughout the two terms during which discussions ran, there were swings between demands for more structure in the groups (making some of them tutorials about the current design projects) and rebellion against structure (what there was of it, such as the regularity of time and place, and particularly the size and composition of the group in order to achieve maximum heterogeneity). Sometimes there was excessive attendance, members of the group who were supposed to attend one session 'invading' the other, and at other times only a few came. As the sessions progressed, the students tended to choose to participate in smaller groups of about six and their discomforts in the new learning situation were brought up even more intensively. Though resenting any infringement of their freedom, they were often unable to take full advantage of it, feeling apathetic and listless, without structure or support. Toward the end of the series, as the examination approached, the staff's conflicts also became clearer – in particular, their feelings about manipulating and transmitting the external demands for certain kinds of performance, or on the other hand about relinquishing control and abandoning the students to chaos. Growth was apparent in the participants' discriminating use of the groups, as they felt freer to attend not at all, or twice in one day, according to their needs. They also began to bring very specific issues to the groups for discussion ...

Design skills
Issues related to design were always prominent in the discussions, especially as design could be seen both as a form of manipulation (and yet we were trying to liberate ourselves and others from being manipulated) and also as the means by which change could be implemented (as indeed we were all manipulating the course) ... There were some intense discussions about blocks to designing: the complexity of decision-making; the difficulty of incorporating technology; the conflicts inherent in creating by destroying; the need for highly personal commitment to design products; and the fear of failure to measure up to aspirations. The staff, too, expressed ambivalent feelings about their changed role. Sometimes staff members were disappointed that the students were less able to produce effective work than under the old system, worried by apathy, poor attendance and lack of commitment; and at other times they were excited by the excellence of some of the design studies.

Professionalism
The students were for some time concerned with their identity as potential architects, because the freedom of the course made them feel a lack of definition of their common objectives. Later there was an increasing concern about presenting themselves in a professional manner and urgent exploring of the implications of the professional role. There was a general rejection of the architectural 'gods', but many students had a strong desire to be accepted by the RIBA into the profession, accompanied by anxieties about being swallowed up by the professional image. Finally, there was a growing confidence in their ability to open the apparently closed doors of professionalism and to develop into the kind of professionals they wanted to be.

Team work
One way of preparing for professional team work was provided by experiencing group interaction in the discussions. In addition, current difficulties in the self-selected project groups were brought up. The essential problems were those of dealing with intra- and inter-group competition, of feeling free as individuals yet functioning in a cohesive unit, and of assessing the group product.

Discussion

Perhaps it is not oversimplifying the issues too much to describe one of the crucial aims of educating for change as that of learning to incorporate the old in order to make the new, of learning how to make the best use of other people's experience, as the basis for one's own innovations. The greater the complexity of the body of knowledge needed by professionals, the greater is their need of free access to the store of experience of experts. However conveniently information may be filed in libraries and made retrievable by computers, there is still much that can at present be got more easily and effectively through personal interaction. This applies especially to technical skills, habits of work, and professional attitudes. Our attempts to provide opportunities for practice in making use of other people's experience did not meet with unqualified success; students did not make maximum use of the staff nor of the consultants to develop their skills in design. This is not to say that the experience did not prepare them to do so in the future. It is likely that it did; but undoubtedly the designs they produced were impoverished by this failure to collaborate fully with all the relevant members of a design team.

The extent to which one individual's experience is openly available to another depends on the inter-personal relationships which they can establish with each other, a function of idiosyncratic constitutions, life histories and ways of thought, all interacting in and with the present situation. We wanted to learn in, and with, the present situation. We wanted to learn how to control these factors in the interest of improving interaction, and not to be commanded by them. In retrospect, it seems that we were handicapped by our failure to define our various roles adequately. Granted that we were all in this together, all learning how to continue to learn, it was confusing to belittle the differences in the parts we needed to play. The staff had special responsibilities for ensuring the success of the project in achieving not only our ultimate educational goals but the immediate goal – for students to qualify for exemption from the RIBA Part II examination within the year . . . But the senior staff did not clearly see where their responsibility should usefully end, nor the younger ones where theirs could most effectively begin. And the students, nominally emancipated from authoritarianism, could not see that they could enrich their own skills by incorporating parts or aspects of the old without prejudice to their new-found liberty.

. . . Even more difficult to come to terms with was the dual role of the staff, who were both teachers and examiners. As the session wore on, this duality deepened and interfered seriously with the participant relationships we intended. One of the many signs was the students' loss of interest in assessing each other's work . . . Nor did the staff members provide serious opportunity for reciprocating assessment (would they have merited even an honorary Diploma from the students?). The interference of examining with teaching was particularly damaging when deliberate attempts were being made to liberate students . . .

Another powerful internal factor to be reckoned with was the inevitable trauma that accompanies change. The wish to be different was accompanied by the fear of being different, and the wish to remain by the fear of getting stuck, or left behind. Such wishes and fears inspired and bedevilled the efforts of students and staff alike, and some of our difficulties in changing could be ascribed to collusions between us to keep things the same . . .

Analysis of Data from Group Discussions: Insights into the Research Process

From 'A contribution to the psychology of designing', *Journal of Architectural Education*, 30, 4, 15–19, 1977.

Much talk, thought and writing have been devoted to the design process in the last two decades . . . In studios everywhere, there has been experimentation in new methods of teaching design. However, risking a generalization, it can be said that attention has been paid mostly to cognitive aspects of the design process . . .

Glimpses of a different aspect of the design process . . . are given by Colman (1974), a psychiatrist exploring some irrational processes which influence physical and social design. He considers basic assumptions – 'the personal and group unconscious and the stereotypic cultural archetypes which influence our behaviour in subterranean and unacknowledged ways' and 'covert politics, the social field of alliances, pressure groups and power influence operating within the design process in unexamined ways, unrelated to the overtly stated design determinants'. Some of the psychological factors which Burgess (1970) discusses in a stimulating paper on ego-involvement in systems designers are relevant also to architects.

The present paper is concerned with similar intangibles, but on a micro scale – with the mundane psychological factors that in unacknowledged and unexamined ways affect the performance of the individual student in the studio. These include his personal habitual ways of thought and action, that specific mix of attitudes, predilections or prejudices, expectations, hopes and aspirations, timidities and fears that are tangled up in his design work, inhibiting or furthering it as the case may be. The lucky student may get help with controlling the effects of these from an intuitive teacher, in treasured one-to-one interaction over the drawing board, but the healing untanglings happen below awareness, and are seldom available to others through verbalization. It is with factors such as these, but brought into the light in conversation, that this paper is concerned. Evidence of them is drawn from relatively unstructured 'free' or 'associative' group discussions (Abercrombie, 1970). Our intention was to help each participant become himself, aware of previously unacknowledged and unexamined aspects of his own behaviour, so that he might better control them. The discussions formed part of a one-year course for the postgraduate Diploma in Architecture. The course was oriented to giving students more responsibility for their own learning than previously, in order to 'educate for change'.

The discussions, each lasting one and a half hours, were held weekly. The class of 25 was divided into two parts, each working with an architect tutor; one group was invited to meet with its tutor and two group conductors (the authors) in the morning and the other in the afternoon of the same day. Audio tape-recordings were made. Attendance was irregular and on a few occasions a student came to both meetings of the day. Sixteen pairs of discussions were held, which are here referred to by serial number. Fictitious names are used for students and tutors, initials JA and PT for the group conductors. The manner of conducting the discussions, and the kind of observation that occurred appear in Abercrombie and Terry (1971). Two of the themes to emerge, the problems of adapting to professional status and adjusting to change in authority-dependency relationships, have been described (Abercrombie and Terry, 1973 [see also Abercrombie and Terry, 1978b]).

For many students, these are closely involved in a third theme which is considered here, their personal problems in designing. From the beginning the group discussions were used to explore design problems. We have assembled some of the relevant statements from the recorded discussions under five main headings, while recognizing that the classification is arbitrary.

The design work on which the students were engaged over the period of the discussions began with a short exercise intended to make a direct contact with the current professional scene. The brief was one for an architectural competition, for a group of 24 flatlets for elderly people in Byfleet, Surrey. This 'closed' problem led to the study of more general, social and ethical problems of housing the elderly. North Kensington, an area of London presenting intensively the urban problems of poverty, sickness, racial strife, delinquency, overcrowding and transport, was the basis for this study. The very narrow and the very loose projects tended to be equally overwhelming and incapacitating; the students felt unable to implement the kinds of change they valued, particularly in the human and socio-economic areas.

Collecting information

The problems deriving from the time lapse between collecting information and designing first arose in the second meeting when Ray said:

> A common difficulty and maybe a criticism that could be levelled against this school is that one is taught to assimilate together great piles of information and get all your sociological data right and then compile those criteria with everything else. What tends to happen is that you do this before you start designing, before you put pen to paper, and you

reach a point where you don't know where to go. I think if you start designing almost straight away in a vacuum, as it were, in a sociological dream, just using your own knowledge and your own common sense, it helps you get into the problem a lot quicker.

He picked up this theme again ten minutes later:

The question of priorities worries me. Aspects of the design which initially were quite high in priority I decided to throw over, because somebody points out how you can handle them differently. Suddenly they cease to have the significance that they had. So many of one's priorities are arbitrary.

It was still worrying students in the second term. In meeting 9 Henry said:

You're not making any ongoing use of the information you collect . . . so everything is relevant in a way, whereas if you're actually working on a project you know what is relevant and what isn't.

Some minutes later Adam confessed:

There was a situation where I felt I made the problem so large and the parameters so tight that I couldn't reconcile that with what I required of my design. I suppose this is the sort of thing that's happening with regard to the North Kensington study.

Later Henry said:

There's a question now in my mind about most of the things that people are trying to find out, whether they aren't the kind of things that people can make assumptions about anyway and then start doing design proposals based on those assumptions.

Adam doubted:

I think it is valid to try to get some kind of understanding of what the real situation in this particular area is. So I think that a lot of this information-finding is quite relevant, but it's not absolutely necessary to do before one starts to think about the problem or about one's own design priorities.

In meeting 13 Graham expressed the conflict again:

You get to a situation where you've got to decide something and you know that you can get more information to help you decide, then you go and find it, or if you can't find it you just decide anyway . . . But if you just decide all the time, it's just fairyland all the time.

Postponing and producing

The issue of producing in design, as distinct from collecting information, arose sharply in meeting 7, triggered by the mid-term reviews in which some groups had merely produced reports. Adam said:

In letting us do exactly what we want there are big opportunities for us to evade solving problems, and I think many groups took that opportunity in stating the problems and analysing them, going into depth and research and so on. If they had nothing fixed to be presented, they could really evade coming onto the most difficult problem of all, which was to try to state some hypothesis, some solution.

Lance disagreed with this censure and argued that they had already spent 'three years always ending up with products, and we're pretty much used to doing that by now'. Adam continued:

I think the important thing in producing is that you actually have to get it out of you, have to put something up which you can then step back from and begin to see what you really did and how it really goes against your beliefs.

Tony emphasized, as Adam had done, the need to 'force' ideas out of oneself, but said:

The danger is in producing something and saying this is great, this is marvellous . . . the danger comes when you think, 'I've finished, I'll go and do something else now'. You have to see it as a continuing thing.

JA referred to expressions of the dilemma in previous meetings and said:

One of the difficulties of decision-making in design . . . [is that] you can sit on the fence so long that you can't get off it; and it's very critical how serious your criticisms of yourself are going to be; you've got to be critical enough to stir you to make a good effort but not so harsh that you can't lift a finger.

Tony extended the problem to the role of the architect:

The problem is so big and so many aspects of it are not directly related to architecture, we feel we're not really qualified . . . the biggest input you've got in a situation like this is your own attitudes . . .

Don said: 'In this open-ended situation I think it's meant a lot of people having to decide "what am I going to do with architecture?" ' Tony continued: 'Until you're willing to make one or two guesses about the way you'd like to move it then you can't really produce anything.' Later, he said: 'The built environment does affect people's behaviour'; and elaborated this:

Then every time you build anything you are affecting people's behaviour so you decide in what ways you want to affect people's behaviour and not just let it happen, or you have to make a positive statement and say I'm just going to let it happen.

After some forty minutes of further discussion around this topic, JA said:

These problems of understanding personal issues of old people, or the committees and all the organizations that you come across – some of you were actually dealing with these problems, as has been said, as a way of postponing commitment to building, as though you'd said, first I'll get straightened out myself and then I'll be a builder... I think you've got to do both at once.

Resistance to changing one's design

In meeting 2, Ray had described how he had thrown over some aspects of his design when someone pointed out they could be handled differently. In meeting 9, resistance to accepting such need for change was discussed. Adam said:

I think it sometimes happens where you have a constraint and you're changing your priorities and so on and you don't notice that the constraint becomes invalidated. I've actually found that I've had buildings with certain things in them the reason for which has disappeared somewhere further along the line and it's had to be pointed out to me.

Henry added:

I think that's often the cause of the blockage too, the fact that you won't let go of something which you thought was good, you can't quite let it go... Let the thing go so that you can build a bigger pattern which includes some new things as well.

JA quoted Picasso as having said that every picture is the sum of destruction, and referred to Clouzot's film of his technique, showing him painting, rubbing out and repainting over and over again. Henry doubted the relevance of this sort of behaviour to architectural design.

It isn't the kind of image which appeals very much to architects... it's not my idea of the architect's mentality... something about the permanence of buildings which are indestructible which I think subconsciously appeals.

Adam recalled the drawbacks of obsessional repetitiveness:

I think the other extreme, from personal experience, can also be destructive. I found this with the old people's home last term, where I went through I don't know how many designs, but I was continually reassessing my priorities... I think I had not enough conviction, or commitment to anything that I'd done...

Later Henry brought up again the frequently recurring theme of the value of testing by designing:

I don't think you do know what's good when you actually sit down and design something. You only know what isn't good and you keep on rejecting it. You explore it and something comes out at the end and when I sit down I reject what I know and try to find something else in the process.

Resistance to incorporating other people's (and especially a tutor's) ideas into one's designs were expressed. For instance, in meeting 2, Dennis said:

I'm at the point where I feel as if all the things which are suggested to me by tutors in my schemes should be coming from within me because it's my design and it's me who's being assessed as a designer at the end of the year . . . and I feel guilty if I accept advice and if I don't accept the advice the scheme probably gets a bad grading or a lower grading.

Jeff asked him: 'Do you feel guilty about taking advice from another student?' Dennis answered: 'Yes, there are times when I feel guilty in a similar manner about walking around the studio looking at other people's schemes.'

In a much later discussion (14) Adam repeated this theme, but added to it the feeling that his own design was being threatened.

I know that I have always felt a degree of resistance to having a tutor who comes along and discusses things with me and maybe makes suggestions about a design I'm doing, because I've always felt that I should be able to do these things for myself . . . and you resist listening to your tutor and you feel that your design is being violated if he comes along and makes a suggestion which objectively may be quite satisfactory.

Later Don referred to this as 'sort of impinging on your . . . creativity'.
In discussion 9 the importance of self-confidence arose, and Henry said:

I can remember last year working on a portrait gallery and Gordon or Bill (studio tutors) would come along and suggest something . . . I would curse them for a solid quarter of an hour after they'd pushed me that way but in the end you go along. It's just a question of building up your emotional attitude adequately and then being able to follow the course that you see is relevant to what you're trying to do.

Aesthetic criteria

In discussion 6, students looked back somewhat resentfully to their early training in the School because they thought the aesthetic element had been frowned upon. Adam expressed a sneaking admiration for those architects who produced 'architects' architecture', and when Bill asked why he felt the need of confidence to 'put over the aesthetic situation', Adam replied that aesthetic had been a dirty word. Russell elaborated this. 'If you tend to do something which is more subjective and just couldn't stand up well to the crit, you made damn sure next time you didn't do it.' Adam agreed: 'We had to justify any formal or aesthetic interest in terms of organization.' Jeff added: 'The only aesthetic possible then was the machine aesthetic.'

The difficulty of visualizing the building one is designing was described by Henry in discussion 16.

The problem for me is that last year we got to talking about and thinking out how a building looks . . . and as soon as you do that, when you design you can't let it proceed until you've seen what it looks like built, because you're kind of getting lost further and further in fantasies. The only way really to refine your design process and your sensibility to other buildings once you get to that stage is for it to be a dialogue between the drawing and the thing built.

The ethics of designing

As was foreshadowed in the citation made from the first meeting, students expressed considerable concern about the ethics of their own objectives in designing. In meeting 3 Henry said:

We somehow allowed ourselves to believe that we were somehow fulfilling the needs of these old people . . . the most important thing about fulfilling one's needs is that one does it oneself and that no one can fulfil someone else's needs . . . it's so excruciatingly patronizing.

Ray said: 'You're working yourself into the position of the non-designer . . . somebody's got to keep the rain out.' Pam said she felt sorry for old people and wanted to give them a high-quality environment. Others supported her, but Henry persisted. 'Because I designed the building, they are unable to fulfil themselves . . . I'm exploiting their needs . . . it's the process of fulfilment that I'm robbing them of.' JA said: 'Isn't there a feeling that you are very unlike them? Because if you do have a certain amount of commonality, what you would want would be helping them.'

Later Tony described a related source of guilt:

talking about self-indulgence, I only design well when I'm enjoying myself . . . I'm worried that this is because it's me that becomes the end product. At the stage . . . when I can't identify with the scheme, I design badly . . . I'm only worried that might take over, that suddenly I'll get a glazed look and enjoy it for the wrong reasons.

In discussion 5, some students showed themselves rethinking their attitudes about what a 'productive' design process might be. Ray said:

Is a productive process thinking about a building? . . . This last couple of weeks we haven't got an awful lot done but it's been a very hard couple of weeks . . . We're not going to have great piles of drawings to pin up tomorrow.

Dennis contrasted this with the following:

The old people's home where we went through and we produced a set of drawings at the end, that was a comfortable feeling . . . it was nice to have actually done something.

Tony added: 'It's nice to hide in, it's nice to design a building once you get going because you can forget things.' Ray agreed: 'An apparently simple decision can be made very early on and you can forget the whole why and wherefore.'

Later Adam came back to the problem of coping with an overwhelming abundance of political, social and psychological data.

> Our group has arrived at a point where we've also been wondering whether any kind of built environment is necessary for this problem; and we've tried to go through a complete reorganization of political and social structures and so on. This obviously is very difficult in such a short time and with such limited knowledge, and we feel that maybe we're just not capable of doing this.

There were many signs of lack of self-confidence. In discussion 7 Leo said:

> I think the architect in getting all these other fields within his realm is beginning to realize that he actually has a great deal of power ... it seems the reason we were all on the fence the last couple of days is that we want the decisions to be made by the people because this at least takes some of the blame off anything that didn't come out right because it's not just you.

In the afternoon of the same day when anxieties about producing were again being expressed, Russell said: 'I just wondered if we're actually scared to put down a building in case it didn't live up to our philosophies.' But in a later discussion (9), Adam faced reality more squarely: 'Maybe it's not possible for us to be designers at all or idealistic ... but we're going to have to reconcile our ideas with certain limitations.'

Discussion 11 was mainly about presentation. There was an overriding sense that students felt they were 'conning' others by presenting a certain design methodology, and making realizations for certain decisions. Russell said of one design team: 'They'd work in a very linear fashion from start to finish and it was very convincing.' James added: 'And everyone else thought that this was the way to get good marks.' Dennis confessed: 'I certainly gave it a try, and I got very frustrated because I didn't work like that at all. It's not such a rational process.' Russell recalled: 'We used to get marks for working method.' Sam, the tutor, said: 'You will do that with a client to justify the decisions you arrived at. It is because you're asked to make an absolute decision in an area where there are no absolutes.' JA said: 'Don't you think you could just tell them that there are arguments this way and that way, but your personal opinion is so and so?' James answered: 'No, because you've got to produce the argument worked backwards from your personal position.' Russell, more confident, said: 'You're more likely to be right than anyone else. Then you've just got to convince people.' Dennis agreed with this, saying: 'So that when you go back to justify it you've made the decision and as far as you can tell it is the right decision, but now you're justifying it to other people.'

Some students were very harsh about 'conning' or 'façadism' in design. In discussion 15, Kay said of a much acclaimed building: 'And you look at it and you think terrific structure, and you go into a bit more detail and actually it's just pure façadism.' Don, referring to a design he had been preparing for an architect, said: 'And he looked at it and he took it away and said, "That's a bit too heavy there, move it up there, add a little weight here", and I said, "But why?" and he said, "That's design!"'

Conclusion

The themes that seemed significant in our discussion included: problems of assimilating (as distinct from merely collecting) information and incorporating it effectively; difficulties of deciding on priorities among criteria; lack of self-confidence in asserting one's subjective aesthetic criteria; the effort required to commit oneself to a design, and the urgent need to provide a tangible test for one's otherwise too vague ideas; possessiveness in design which gives rise to barriers against changing one's design – to destroy in order to create – with changing evaluations of intentions and constraints, and to stubborn resistance to alternatives; guilt about self-indulgence in enjoyment of the act of designing; and fear of being trapped into 'conning'.

The question arises as to how common these problems are. The students whose conversation is cited, each with his individual personal characteristics, with various levels and kinds of competence in designing, were a fairly representative sample of those whom we have known at the Bartlett School of Architecture, over some ten years, and we have no reason to suppose they are not shared by those at other schools undergoing similar developments (Abercrombie, 1974). We do not have any evidence that talking about such difficulties in small groups, in the way described, either immediately or ultimately improves the participants' performance in design. However, JA suggested one way in which group discussion might facilitate designing:

> One of the things that strikes me over and over again is the difficulty of imagining what the building is going to be like from a number of different viewpoints . . . it's this multiplicity of views that is encouraged in group discussions. You are by analogy able to take another person's position, to switch about in your viewpoint of what is going on . . .

Improving Small Group Teaching: Tutors' Concerns

From M.L.J. Abercrombie and P.M. Terry, *Talking to Learn: improving teaching and learning in small groups.* London: Society for Research into Higher Education, Chapter 11 ('Themes'), 1978.

In [the following] an attempt will be made to generalize about the content of the wide range of group discussions we have had with teachers and students on small-group teaching. Though our discussion groups have been very various, and though successive meetings of the same group may differ very much, it is possible to draw out some themes which recurred frequently. They were differently treated by different groups, and by the same group from time to time, various aspects of the same theme being taken up, and in relationship to a variety of others.

The teaching groups concerned

The group situations that teachers and students (in different departments and institutions) discussed were quite varied. The tutorials or seminars, as they were variously called, consisted of between four and fifteen students, but were mostly of between six and eight. A teacher was usually engaged with the same group for several weekly or fortnightly meetings over a term or a session, but in a few cases met a group only two or three times. Sometimes a whole class was small enough to be tutored as a unit; more often it was divided among several tutors, in which case apparently little was done to attempt any kind of standardization. It did not seem common for teachers to combine in tutorials, or to visit each other's, or to have much discussion about the rationale of the various administrative arrangements, for instance as to the size of group, frequency of meeting, whether of stable or changing constitution, whether the tutors should be constant or rotating. Often participants in our discussions had not had other opportunities of discussing their teaching with colleagues, and only in a very few cases had teachers discussed their intentions or methods with their students.

The tutorials were always more or less related to the content of the syllabus, that is the material that would be tested in final examinations, but how narrowly or broadly the topic was defined varied greatly and was much discussed, as we shall see later. The basis for class discussion might be a previous lecture, given by the tutor or another teacher, the tutorial being offered as an opportunity for students to bring up difficulties, confusions, or misunderstandings. In one intensive discussion of a tutor's problems in conducting a group based on another teacher's lectures, it was pointed out that discussion might be easier if the focus seemed less threatening than that of dealing with failures of understanding, if for instance the tutor asked what positive gains the students had made from the lecture rather than what difficulties had been encountered. In most cases the discussion was focused on previous reading by the students of a passage of prose . . . an article from a learned journal . . . or their translation of a passage from English into another language or vice versa . . .

One of the main problems was that of getting students to prepare themselves in advance for the tutorial. A natural response of the teacher was to save embarrassment by giving a summary of what the students ought to have read. But this, however well intentioned and however comforting to the delinquent, tended to encourage further slackness and dependency on the students' part. One of the beneficial results of video-taping classes and subsequently discussing them was the insight this gave to students and teachers about the stultifying effects of their illusive behaviour. Teachers could modify their desire to be all-providing and students their school-bred notion that homework is done mostly to please teacher. Students were stimulated to make greater efforts to do it in order to profit from and enjoy the tutorial.

An example of the way the lecturer-listener mode of teaching tended to carry over into what was intended to be a discussion session was that students often came to the class with pencil and notepaper, but without their own notes on the passage, and even without the passage itself to refer back to and notate. By contrast, in the situation shown in the peer tutoring video-tape [see Abercrombie and Terry, 1978a: Ch. 6] the table was covered with students' scripts and reference books, and there was constant checking back and forth, attention being paid as much to the written words as to the discussion about them.

In a few cases a paper prepared by a student was intended to form the basis for discussion, and here the main problem was that of involving the class. Too often a student who had prepared the paper stepped into the shoes of the authoritative tutor, the others encouraged by relative ignorance to take only a passive role. The possibility of setting up a debating situation, in which two students presented opposing views (which might or might not be their own) on a given topic was sometimes suggested. This seems, however, to have rather limited application to small groups. On the other hand, peer tutoring offers innumerable opportunities for the discussion of alternative hypotheses (usually more than two) about small points.

Assessment of students

Because most small-group classes were syllabus-oriented the problem of student assessment often arose. It was often argued that if small-group tutorials were to be taken seriously as part of the curriculum and attendance at them required, or at least expected, then students should be graded on their performance and the marks used in the final assessment for the degree. Two strong objections were commonly raised. One was the technical difficulty of grading people in so open a situation, in which variations in personality play a prominent role. Clearly a talkative student offers himself for assessment (for good or ill) more easily than a silent one whose reasons for saying nothing are inscrutable – they may be that he is thinking too hard, with too many points to consider, or thinking not at all, consumed with shyness, or inhibited by ignorance or stupidity.

It was usually agreed that students could be judged on what written work they had done in relation to the discussions (whether in preparation for them or in retrospect). By contrast, in most discussions it was not possible to assess what all students had learned or how much or what they had contributed to the group. A silent member, for instance, might contribute a lot by supplying the necessary stimulus of a listener. It cannot be supposed, however, that a teacher will be unaffected in his grading of a student's script by the behaviour he has witnessed in class. In peer tutoring . . . a tutor found that she had been able to mark and comment on scripts more efficiently and with much greater interest after hearing the discussion. As to the students, each participant is continuously and automatically judging his own and others' contributions. Indeed, that participation in interactive groups offers such rich opportunities for the exercise of discrimination is one of its greatest advantages over more passive ways of learning.

A second objection to assessment came up: while students might take tutorials more seriously if they thought that their performance was being graded, they might also be inhibited by it, not daring to risk making mistakes. This might have a deleterious effect on their learning. The social climate of a group in which assessment for administrative purposes was taking place would be very different from one whose attention was focused on learning. The students would see the tutor in an ambiguous position, as simultaneously teacher and examiner, rather than in both roles at different times. And for his part the tutor might find his attention divided between his two roles. In general, therefore, most teachers thought it not only too difficult, but inexpedient to award grades to students for performance in group discussion.

Control of content

The question as to how much departure from a narrowly defined topic should be permitted or encouraged was a matter of very great concern to both teachers and students. Nobody doubted that students were at university to get degrees, and as good degrees as possible, and that getting a degree involved 'covering the syllabus'. Most people felt that 'covering the syllabus' was better done (or at least appeared to be so) by listening to lectures, or reading prescribed passages, or doing set exercises, than by discussing. It is difficult for teachers accustomed to the lecture system to forgo the lecture mode in tutorial classes which require a different style. A linear sequence of argument can be sustained by one person speaking uninterruptedly and, if he is a sufficiently riveting lecturer, a large number of listeners can follow him step by step. The small group offers a medium for a different kind of teaching and learning. Thought develops quite otherwise in interactive discussion, changing in pace and duration, often diverging, running into a blind alley or quite off the map, often backtracking, revising, clarifying, enlarging and enriching a point that may have seemed settled already. One teacher, in studying the video-tape of one of his classes, realized how too rigid adherence to his preformed logical plan for the seminar had led him to reject a student's contribution that came inconveniently out of order, and in so doing had dampened class participation . . .

Technical difficulties apart, many teachers and students believe that higher education involves something more than covering the syllabus. As one teacher said: 'Surely this is part of the learning process, to wander down a few blind alleys of our own choosing?' A significant brief passage occurred between three students in the Scandinavian Studies class during a discussion on art: 'You've got to come to some kind of definition of the poet's art.' A second said: 'A discussion like that is surely what university is all about.' A third student commented that 'it sort of petered out', which the second explained was because 'we were worried about not keeping up with the syllabus'. In another group a sociologist said: 'One's discipline is a social-ization into other ways of enquiry rather than simply having ingested a lot of knowledge', and a physiologist:

> I suppose that one of one's objectives is that when students have com-pleted the course, they'll be able to look back on it as a fairly satisfac-tory experience, so that one shouldn't necessarily define their objectives simply in terms of getting through examinations. It is, as it were, a sort of growing-up process which a lot of people go through when they come straight from school, and simply just learning to speak in a group helps them to speak in semi-public situations.

So the problem seemed to be how to make a partial covering of the syllabus the medium for a 'liberal education'; and the breadth of the latter was itself differently interpreted. It included making possible what some students of Chaucer yearned for . . . a deeper and richer understanding of the *Prologue* than they could get from studying that work alone – they needed knowledge of its relation to other works of Chaucer and indeed to the great body of literature in general, and of the historic and social context in which it was written. For students of language, it included getting a glimmer of understanding of some grand principles of linguistics, through struggle with the minutiae of translating a few sentences of English into French.

For some teachers it was still wider: to quote a linguist, it 'is not only finding out about the content of a course in a narrow sense, but finding out about the institution in which he is doing it and what the constraints are and the world within which that institution is, and why the hell he is doing it at all'. For some it included the mastery of self-direction, growth of the ability to continue to learn, the fostering of personal development. If this aspect of learning is taken to the extreme we tend to veer towards moral tutoring, or counselling, or psychotherapy. Many teachers consider it part of their job to concern themselves with students' personal problems – at least with those that block the way to 'covering the syllabus'. One teacher, another linguist, considered the possibility of running special discussions for the students 'just to get all sorts of worries, problems, puzzles and things off their minds'. This is one solution, the separation in time and place, but with the same tutor, of 'personal' and 'academic' aspects of development. But the teacher whose main aim is to broaden, deepen and enrich the students' understanding of the substance of the academic curriculum is still faced with the problem of how much structure, how much freedom to provide within the discussion period. Examples of pertinent discussion of this dilemma are given in [Abercrombie and Terry, 1978a: Ch. 3], where students questioned their tutor about his control. In discussing the video-tape one teacher commented: 'You bound their freedom to give them security, that's what they're asking you for', and another asked later: 'How much structure should be given to allow their freedom? At what point can you remove the structure because they make their own structure?'

Control of participation

Over and above the difficulties of getting any sort of discussion going, the problems of how to restrain the too dominating student, or how to help the silent to articulate at all, recurred frequently among teachers' groups, whether small or large. The roots of the symptoms were in the teacher's anxiety to make the party go ('I just assumed that small-group discussions should be full of discussion, noise and action'). The practiced lecturer found it difficult to tolerate a silence, and rushed to fill it with easy fluency while students, much less ready with tongue, needed time to formulate, to stumble and hesitate. The teacher needed to open his ears rather than his mouth, to show signs of wanting to listen and understand and of having heard and noted. The same anxiety resulted in the teacher encouraging the verbally fluent, opinionated student to dominate. Such was his relief at finding one who had done his homework and wanted to talk about it that he engaged in a dialogue, making it more difficult for any others to join in, whether with himself in another dialogue, or with other students. The other students might tend to collude with this; however suppressed, irritated or bored they felt about 'big-mouth', at least he released them from the obligation to rouse themselves, and anyway they might actually learn from the substance of the dialogue. As for the silent students, many teachers found them embarrassing, partly out of a wish that all should be equal, because their objective of helping students to express themselves was being frustrated, or because an obstinate silence was mystifying and threatening. In [Abercrombie and Terry, 1978a: Ch. 3] teachers exchanged hints on how to bring the silent student in; and in [1978a: Chs 4 and 5] another told how he learned of non-verbal methods of helping: 'You just look directly towards the students, catch their eye and move your hand a bit.' Another generalized about the importance of non-verbal communication: 'It doesn't matter what we say but what we do.'

Students, of course, accepted the view that the control of the direction of discussion, its pace, and allotment of time for contributions, was the teacher's job. It was with some surprise that from the study of video-tapes of their own class, students came to recognize their potentialities for control . . . They could themselves help the shy student to talk, or the too voluble to restrain himself. It took time for all to realize that their collusive behaviour was producing results that were undesirable but could be redirected to achieve their declared aims more effectively.

Student–teacher relationships

Teaching in small groups obviously offers opportunities for relationships of a more social kind between participants than does the lecture system. Some teachers felt uneasy at softening the division between the professional and personal aspects of themselves, and some students also preferred to maintain social distance. The absence of an accepted code of behaviour in apparently quite simple matters such as how to address students was clear in [Abercrombie and Terry, 1978a: Ch. 8]. The influence of physical context on social climate was recognized (for example, in [1978a: Ch. 2]). The classroom itself was in some cases felt to impose restraints, sometimes helpful, sometimes deleterious, so that both students and teachers needed to adjust when meeting each other extra-murally. Drinking together in a pub might ameliorate the classroom climate; it might or might not have ultimately beneficial effects on the mental work that went on there.

Authority and dependency

Basic to all problems of teaching and learning is the individual's status as a dependent or as an authority. Among all animal species man is outstanding in the slowness of his physical development, with prolonged dependence on adults as foetus, infant and child, for biological survival; in his ability to continue to develop mentally; and in the essentially social nature of his learning. The change from a state of partial parasitism to that of being responsible for one's own welfare and for others' is difficult enough in most societies. For those who undertake prolonged formal 'higher' education, there are particular troubles as well as pleasures and privileges. The change in status is patchy. The student is physically mature, and is recognized by the state as socially responsible . . . but is still not self-maintaining. He comes to be taught by people who are not only authorities in the fields of learning he has chosen, but who are in authority over him as examiners, and possibly in due course as arbiters of at least the beginnings of his career.

It is not surprising that there are commonly strong streaks of dependency in students' attitudes to their tutors, however self-assertive and rebellious they may be from time to time, and some at most times. Some demand that lectures should be stimulating; they are not enthused by the subject itself, but need to receive it through a charismatic channel. Many are not self-motivated to work, or not sufficiently so, and need their teacher to encourage, cajole or goad them into it. They work less to please themselves, than to please teacher. One of these students said: 'I think the leaders of a seminar have definitely got the right to expect all the students to have done a fair amount of work in preparation for each seminar.' A teacher commented that some students seemed to offer written work to her as a gift: 'That's the way the student gives it and is extremely resentful if I'm not duly grateful.' Another remarked that the attitude 'isn't always necessarily "am I giving the right answer about Voltaire or about hydrogen chloride?". It's often of the nature of "am I behaving the right way, teacher?"' An example of how, during the course of a few weekly discussions, some students of Education changed in their perceptions of themselves as students and prospective teachers is briefly reported elsewhere (Abercrombie 1970; in this volume, see pp. 82–3). In the present project, too, some students not only moved towards accepting responsibility for their own learning but planned to make their experience available to their successors.

Teachers also have their problems – of their relationship to authorities, of being authorities themselves, and of their relationship to students whom they must wean from dependence. The teacher's (especially the young teacher's) relationship to seniors in his department and institution is not unlike that of his students to himself – he is dependent on them for learning (in his case not only in his subject, but the way the administration works) and may be dependent on their good will for promotion. One of these teachers told how in his first job he was advised to lecture quickly, to cover a lot of ground, 'and it took two years of the students telling me I was going too fast to alter. I thought he must be right – he's a professor, he's an expert.'

Quite often, teachers are constrained in teaching what and how they would like by what they perceive as arbitrary and unchangeable rules about curriculum and examinations. It took these teachers time and thought to discover, with the support of the group, that they could do a lot to improve their own teaching by slight changes in their own behaviour, without offending their colleagues or toppling the structure of the institution. It was a matter of evaluating more realistically their own and others' powers and limitations. Analogically, in a discussion group they might perceive the conductor as all-powerful and unchallengeable, enforcing rigid rules of behaviour which were actually a reflection of their own.

As to their own status as authorities in the subject they are teaching, the teachers felt less self-confident than was comfortable; they experienced a need to tower above their students. This is much discussed in [Abercrombie and Terry, 1978a: Ch. 10] (for example 'I think it's quite a problem if at the beginning of the course you have to say "I don't know" to a lot of questions, then you're really undermining your position for the rest of the year'; 'I think it's basically not feeling self-assured enough to admit error; not feeling self-confident enough, so that I need students to say "goodness, what a lot she knows, she must be good"). The discussions also gave insight into students' feelings of inadequacy and how the teachers might provoke them. One teacher said: 'I presuppose they have a certain knowledge of the material – I don't like it when they don't remember it all. That must make it threatening for them to admit that they don't understand – I've just realized that. It's not much wonder sometimes if they don't talk much in seminars.' A second joined in: 'It's very tempting just to say "haven't you had this in lectures? Surely you've heard about that?"' and a third: 'Particularly "don't you remember me telling you?"'

As to the teacher's activities in renouncing his role of total, all-embracing authority, and weaning the student away from complete dependence upon him, that was the central aim of the project. As is amply illustrated in their discussions, the teachers' struggle was that of being authoritative in their own disciplines, without being authoritarian in behaviour with students, so that they could inform, guide and correct where necessary, but without confining or inhibiting the students' own learning activities.

In encouraging the discussion of some of these basic and controversial themes in higher education we did not see our function as that of getting members of the group to come to agreement, but rather of increasing their awareness of problems and their competence in tackling them. Alternative responses were exposed and explored, but no decision was taken by the whole group. The intention was to help each participant to prepare himself to come to his own decision, the decision most appropriate to specific requirements at specific times and in specific situations.

Using Video-tapes to Improve Teaching in Small Groups

From M.L.J. Abercrombie and P.M. Terry, *Introduction: Learning in Groups: Scripts for Video-tapes*. London: University Teaching Methods Unit, 1974.

I've been thinking about my seminars a lot and what's been going wrong. That's partly why I've got to see these video-tapes. I saw a lot of myself in that teacher on the tape. I tried a different approach this week and I feel much happier and more comfortable.

The value of these tapes and subsequent discussion was for me hearing differing – and in some ways contradictory – views on the role and function of discussion groups and their various aspects. This is helping me to establish my own view.

I *used* to feel that students were so much fodder.

These comments are from teachers who viewed and discussed some of the tapes in this series. We quote them because they express much of the learning that we hope the tapes will encourage: increased awareness of one's own teaching behaviour through identification with material in the tapes, recognizing ways of behaving that are different from one's own, trying out alternatives, gaining in self-confidence and enjoyment, and feeling differently about student–teacher relationships.

The series of video-tapes has been prepared as part of our work on improving small-group teaching, supported by a grant from the University Grants Committee. They are based on material from two aspects of our work. One of these was conducting small-group meetings of teachers discussing their own experiences of group teaching . . . [Abercrombie and Terry, 1978a; in this volume, see pp. 103–11 and 153–60]. Another activity was with individual teachers and their groups of students. Classes were recorded in the classroom or in the television studio; students and teacher came to the studio, usually the following week, to view the recording and to discuss their reactions to it with one of us. Sometimes these discussions also were recorded, and sometimes the class was recorded again some weeks later, or the same teacher was recorded with a new class. The video-tapes were intended primarily for the benefit of the class itself, but in some cases the class had put its tapes to further use (for example, showing them to new students). In three cases, with permission of the classes concerned, parts of the tapes have been incorporated into our series.

For large audiences, Paul Terry conducted discussions stimulated by the showing of excerpts from video-tapes . . . This activity was most successful when run as a short course of four or so weekly meetings, during which a climate of confidence could develop. When 'one-off' shows were given, whether as an isolated event or as part of a conference, personal reactions to the general context affected responses to the presentation.

. . . We would like to illustrate the ways in which our objectives in encouraging use of the video-tapes were met, by further quotations from some recorded discussions among teachers, when they were viewing the tapes on one of our courses, which met for five weekly one-and-a-half-hour sessions. Twenty to thirty people were present.

Teachers are often able to see similarities with their own experience, regardless of discipline, and, as the following quotations (from different teachers) show, to see the way patterns of behaviour become established:

> I'd speak up for the lecturer in that situation and say that if there is a non-participating audience one drones on. It gets a bit of a vicious circle, if you can't get some response one tends to fill the gap.

> The trouble is that the teacher on the tape interprets immediately what each student says. I'm sure I do this too, that's why I noticed it critically. Leaping in and saying 'you mean such-and-such' instead of giving other students time to come in on that plane, he remoulds it into his language straight away.

We think it is useful for the audience to explore alternative ways of behaving. The following discussion was between five members of the audience:

> *Speaker 1*: I was trying to think how I would handle it and I was very very unsure really. But I think there are two things one might do: one might simply change the direction of the discussion by deliberately bringing in . . .
> *Speaker 2*: Could you not just let it go? OK, the student has said something wrong, just let that go.
> *Speaker 3*: Then you get silence.
> *Speaker 4*: Wait for him to be corrected by the way the discussion comes round.
> *Speaker 5*: Might it be possible to reformulate what he said without saying . . . ?

Teachers often relate the discussion to their own experiences:

> Actually this happened to me last week. I began with a certain group for the first time with a student who could not stop talking in spite of the fact that I tried to . . .

On one occasion I tried to get a group involved in putting forward what they expected from the topic at the beginning . . .

Often the discussion extends to broad educational problems, for example, of assessment [see, in this volume, p. 155].

Another important general topic is the student–teacher relationship. (From a teacher in the last session of the course):

> . . . the earlier tapes illustrated the process . . . we've commented on how much more successful [the geography teacher] was, how much warmer and unafraid and so on . . . I'd say that my relationship with my students is much more real people to real people than it was before.

The tapes also demonstrate how the students model their behaviour on the teacher's example:

> I got the impression that the people taking part, particularly the guy who did most of the talking, was trying to imitate the teacher inasmuch as the teacher went off on his great long diatribe and as soon as the dominant guy could get in he didn't want to let go.

> It's very central, isn't it, to how the seminar will go because people will model according to the lecturer. It doesn't matter what we say but what we do.

Similarly, the manner of conducting the viewing-discussion session also serves as a model. Just as we think it is inappropriate for the teacher to dominate a small group, so we feel the video-tape should not dominate discussion. We usually stop the recording after eight short intervals (of ten to fifteen minutes, or at request from the audience) to encourage discussion.

> It seems to me that Paul (Terry) has structured these sessions for us. He has something very much in mind that he's trying to achieve. He's bringing certain materials to each of these sessions and as a result he gives us a certain direction and then he gives us pretty much free rein to go in the direction we want. That's what I mean by structure. It's not constraining structure, it's facilitating structure. Well, if it's possible for a seminar leader to actually produce a series of stimulating ideas the students themselves will get kind of turned on by it . . .

We also hope that the video-tapes will encourage teachers to record and discuss their own classes with students and perhaps other teachers. One of the teachers whose class was recorded commented:

> I found it most exhilarating all the way through this experience. It has taught me a great deal, the course and also the video-taping and discussing after taping the class. This made me mature as a teacher, helped me in the business of doing without an authority figure above me.

A spin-off of the work of one teacher who made some video-tapes has been that all the tutors in his department who run first-year group discussion classes are using parts of his recordings to show to their groups. We feel an important use of tapes is in stimulating students to think about their own active learning in groups. Some have suggested slightly modified roles for the teacher:

> In a discussion if you gave us the facts in a handout, as the teacher, you will still have a wider knowledge, you've read far more, you know more . . . so if we're having an equal discussion it's still bound to be slightly unbalanced, but you should be able to act as a catalyst there. I think if we are better informed to start with it might go a little better.

One student commented on his difficulty in speaking:

> If I've got to be thinking several steps ahead before I say anything, I'm going to be very careful about what I say. I may not say very much, if anything at all. Whereas if I think we can just go through my thought pattern in the discussion, and if I think you (the teacher) are not attacking me, then I'll do that.

Another student expressed his astonishment at the suggestion that he could take an initiative:

> You mean to say that *I* can do something to encourage quiet students to speak, to make the class go better?

Comments are not always favourable:

> I've never seen such a rambling, disorganized discussion in my life.

> They're just waiting for the camera to come their way so they can perform.

Some people object to the tapes because they think the behaviour shown is unrepresentative, owing to the artificiality of video-recording conditions, and others that it is inappropriate for 'my own subject'. Such reactions are nearly always, in our experience, counter-balanced by equally extreme but enthusiastic ones from other members of the audience. Some people do not come back after the first session of a course, others stay on.

Undoubtedly some people by nature find it easier than others to teach and learn effectively in groups. But there is nothing mystical about it; we firmly believe that the skills can be developed and improved and that video-taping is one way of facilitating the process. There seem to be a significant number of teachers and students who can learn from this material, whatever its shortcomings, and who are stimulated to record and discuss their own classes.

The Use of Seminars in Training for Group Work

From 'The seminar: Cambridge Group Work General Course', *Group Analysis*, 18, 1, 36–43, 1985.

In Cambridge we have tackled the difficulties of combining theoretical teaching and experiential work in courses on group work training by drawing theoretical issues out of participants' own practical experience as they describe it in seminars.

Lintott and Speirs (1982) have described the development of the group work course in Cambridge. At present it consists of weekly meetings over three terms of ten weeks. In the first and third terms, seminar groups of eight to ten people meet for one and a half hours, then join the rest of the class for tea before meeting in different sets for small-group experience. During the second term the seminars are replaced by a Large Group . . . Our first General Course, in 1980–1, was based on the London Institute of Group Analysis Course, with the traditional series of nineteen lectures on theory, and small-group experience not explicitly related to the substance of the lectures. Then, in 1981–2, we decided to try to teach 'theory' through seminars.

In the seminar groups, the course begins with students who are not well acquainted interviewing each other in pairs and then presenting each other to the group. They talk about anything that would help them to work together during the coming months – why they want to join the course, what they expect to get out of it, what they most look forward to, what vague fears and anxieties they may have. As each person is presented by his partner he is asked if he or she wishes to add or retract anything, and members ask further questions of interviewer or interviewee, or make comments. In this way each person breaks the 'silence ice', having something to say which will be useful to the group, and may find it easier subsequently to talk spontaneously. The conductor offers to answer any questions put to him.

We do not usually finish the round of presenting everybody in the first meeting and continue in the next. We also make a point of recalling what we learnt about each other last time. This recalling of what happened in the previous week continues throughout the course. It serves to sharpen awareness. Differences of recall naturally occur between different people. The value of other people's recollections is appreciated, and the importance of the group history is emphasized. It also allows individuals to affirm or correct or add to what was said about them.

For the rest of the second meeting, and in the following eight or so meetings, members in turn talk about their own group work, often concentrating on the most recent meeting attended. Members need quite a lot of encouragement to present their groups, and one of the great delights of this kind of learning is to see them grow in confidence and responsibility through the term. During the exposition, other members comment and question. From this, a good impression is gained of the significant aspects of each person's 'group situation' – number of members, staff, institution, length of meeting, frequency, beginning and ending, preparing for breaks and so on. It is striking that many members seem to get very little opportunity at work of discussing their group work with colleagues. It seems to be generally accepted that this is not essential – even for the training of psychiatric nurses!

At the end of the autumn term, I run over each of the cases again, picking out the significant theoretical points as I have seen them, comparing and contrasting the different situations in which people work, the constraints, their different attitudes and basic assumptions about their aims. Opportunity is given for people to contradict or modify what I have said of their performance. It seems that some sort of summary is felt to be useful before breaking for Christmas, and before switching to the Large Group. In the spring term, the seminar leaders attend the Large Group with course members and participate as they wish. In the summer term, members return to the seminars and are in turn invited to present a topic of theoretical interest. In one seminar of the 1983–4 course, in the first meeting, two members collaborated to present the conductor's role, a third acting as timekeeper. In the second meeting, one talked about transparency and opacity in leadership style. In the third, a matter that had arisen during the autumn term was dealt with. A psychiatric nurse in training had described her group of nurses as unsatisfactory because of the behaviour of two leaders (it seemed the main difficulty had been about boundaries). The group had folded up, and a second attempt to reform had also been unsuccessful. The member was encouraged to try again, herself. She giggled in embarrassment when it was suggested she could start it, though she had repeatedly said her group would probably get on better without a staff facilitator. It had never occurred to her to take on the responsibility. With a lot of encouragement she agreed to get out a plan of membership, time, place, frequency of meetings, to discuss it with her colleagues, and then present it to us the next week. The newly re-established group continued to meet.

In Bill Lintott's parallel seminar group, a selection of topics arising from the autumn term discussions were compiled by the group. These were written on cards and placed in the middle of the circle whenever the group was considering which to take next. Topics included starting the group, styles of conducting, working with a co-therapist, boundary issues such as time, confidentiality and so on, group processes such as mirror reactions and resonance, therapeutic factors, and endings. New cards were added as new topics arose during the term.

David Brodie recorded the issues that arose during the first term in the seminar group he was conducting. These were: attitudes to authority (the seminar had considered a group of intermediate treatment offenders whose very reason for being a group meant conflict with authority); 'Why do I get ill?' as a constant theme in a group; the conductor leaving a group because of job change; members fearing that a conductor would talk to outsiders about them; the consequences of a sudden change in a group's format; the way in which a leader behaves and is perceived by members (a hospital group had been away on holiday and became perturbed when one leader appeared at breakfast in her nightdress) . . .

Differences between Lecture and Seminar Methods

To summarize: on this course, the main differences between the lecture and seminar methods of transmitting a body of theoretical knowledge lie in the context in which each is undertaken:

1. In the lecture system there is an asymmetrical relationship between teacher and taught . . . In the seminar system, understanding of theory arises out of the students' own experiences. Active participation is ensured by the group members' need to express themselves, and to test their own understanding by comparison and contrast with that of other members. All are both teachers and students.
2. The lecture system encourages and deepens the split between theory and practice. There is not a one-to-one relationship between the two . . . 'There's nothing so useful as a good theory', as Kurt Lewin said. It is the integration of theory with practice that matters, and this is achieved in the seminar system.
3. We are aware of the influence of transference on relationships within the group, but we do not analyse it. We try to reduce the distance between the teacher and pupil – 'becoming transparent' in Yalom's (1975) phrase. Our aim, exemplified largely by non-verbal means, is to encourage self-confidence in the group members, so that they become autonomous learners, and more resourceful and competent as practitioners. This requires a loosening of the dependency bond between conductor and members, and a strengthening of the allegiances between members, as happens in the intimacies of sharing work experiences. We hope that after the course peer interaction will continue in the Cambridge Group Work Associates, formed by those who have taken the General Course.
4. We differentiate between independence and detachment. We are dealing with relatively normal people, like ourselves . . . I like to think we are

experiencing something of what Foulkes meant when he described group analysis as a social force, recognizing man as a social animal whose personal development is very long – nine months in the womb and ninety years learning to live outside it – and who is required to be emancipated from dependency while maintaining attachment.

Bibliography

Abelson, P.H. (1965) 'Relation of group activity to creativity in science', *Daedalus*, 94, 603–14.

Abercrombie, M.L.J. (1960) *The Anatomy of Judgement*. London: Hutchinson.

Abercrombie, M.L.J. (1964) 'Non-verbal communication', in Renfrew, C. and Murphy, K. (eds) *The Child Who Does Not Talk*. London: Spastics Society/Heinemann, 16–21.

Abercrombie, M.L.J. (1965) 'The nature and nurture of architects', *Transactions of the Bartlett Society*, 2, 53–82.

Abercrombie, M.L.J. (1966) 'Small groups', in Foss, B. (ed.) *New Horizons in Psychology*. Harmondsworth: Penguin, 381–95.

Abercrombie, M.L.J. (1967) 'Psychology and the student', *American Institute of Architects Journal*, 48, 3, 89–92.

Abercrombie, M.L.J. (1969) *The Anatomy of Judgement*. Harmondsworth: Penguin.

Abercrombie, M.L.J. (1970) *Aims and Techniques of Group Teaching*, 1st edn. London: Society for Research into Higher Education.

Abercrombie, M.L.J. (1972) 'Teaching in small groups', in Butcher, H.J. and Rudd, E. (eds) *Contemporary Problems in Higher Education*. London: McGraw-Hill.

Abercrombie, M.L.J. (1974) 'Improving the education of architects', in Collier, K.G. (ed.), *Innovation in Higher Education*. London: National Foundation for Educational Research.

Abercrombie, M.L.J. (1976a) 'The difficulties of changing', in *Health Care in a Changing Setting: the UK experience*. Ciba Foundation Symposium 43 (new series). Amsterdam: Elsevier (Excerpta Medica).

Abercrombie, M.L.J. (1976b), 'Architecture: psychological aspects', in Krauss, S. (ed.) *Encyclopaedic Handbook of Medical Psychology*. London: Butterworth.

Abercrombie, M.L.J. (1977a) 'A contribution to the psychology of designing', *Journal of Architectural Education*, 30, 4, 15–18.

Abercrombie, M.L.J. (1977b) 'Staff development through and for small group teaching', in Elton, L. and Simmonds, K. (eds) *Staff Development in Higher Education*. London: Society for Research into Higher Education.

Abercrombie, M.L.J. (1989) *The Anatomy of Judgement*. London: Free Association Books.

Abercrombie, M.L.J. and Terry, P.M. (1971) 'The first session: an introduction to associative group discussion', in *Aims and Techniques of Group Teaching* (2nd edn). London: Society for Research into Higher Education.

Abercrombie, M.L.J. and Terry, P.M. (1973) 'Students' attitudes to professionalism as seen in group discussion', *Universities Quarterly*, 27, Autumn, 465–74.

Abercrombie, M.L.J. and Terry, P.M. (1974) *Learning in Groups: scripts for videotapes*. London: University Teaching Methods Unit.

Abercrombie, M.L.J. and Terry, P.M. (1978a) *Talking to Learn: improving teaching and learning in small groups*. London: Society for Research into Higher Education.

Abercrombie, M.L.J. and Terry, P.M. (1978b) 'Reactions to change in the authority-dependency relationship', *British Journal of Guidance and Counselling*, 6, 82–94.

Abercrombie, M.L.J. and Terry, P.M. (1979) *Aims and Techniques of Group Teaching*, 4th edn. London: Society for Research into Higher Education.

Abercrombie, M.L.J., Forrest, A.J. and Terry, P.M. (1970) 'Diploma project 1968–69', *Architectural Research and Teaching*, 1, 6–12.

Abercrombie, M.L.J., Gardiner, P.A., Hansen, E., Jonckheere, J., Lindon, R.L., Solomon, G., Tyson, M.C. (1964) 'Visual perceptual and visuomotor impairments in physically handicapped children', *Percepual and Motor Skills*, Suppl. 18, 561.

Abercombie, M.L.J., Terry, P. M. *et al.* (1972) 'Whatever happened to group dynamics?', in *Varieties of Group Discussion in University Teaching*. London: University Teaching Methods Unit.

Ames, A. (1955) *An Interpretative Manual for the Demonstrations in the Psychology Research Centre*. Princeton, NJ: Princeton University Press.

Argyle, M. (1967) *The Psychology of Interpersonal Behaviour*. Harmondsworth: Penguin.

Barnett, S.A. (1958), 'An experiment with free discussion groups', *Universities Quarterly*, 12, 175–80.

Beard, R., Healey, E. and Holloway, P. (1968) *Objectives in Higher Education*. London: Society for Research into Higher Education.

Blackburn, R.T. (1968) 'Live and learn? A look at students in their setting', *Memo to the Faculty No 32*, Centre for Research on Learning and Teaching, University of Michigan.

Bloom, B.S. (ed.) (1954) *Taxonomy of Educational Objectives, Cognitive Domain*. New York: McKay.

Bloom, B.S. (ed.) (1956) *Taxonomy of Educational Objectives, Affective Domain*. New York: McKay.

Bradford, L.P., Gibb, J.R. and Berne, K.D. (eds) (1964) *Group Therapy and Laboratory Method: innovation in re-education*. New York: Wiley.

Broadbent, G. (1973) *Design in Architecture*. London: Wiley.

Burgess, J.H. (1970) 'Ego involvement in the systems design process', *Human Factors*, 12, 7–12.

Cantril, H., Ames, A., Hastorf, A. and Ittleson, W. (1949) 'Psychology and scientific research', *Science*, 110, 461–4.

Caws, P. (1969) 'The structure of discovery', *Science*, 116, 1375–80.

Collier, K.G. (1966) 'An experiment in university teaching', *Universities Quarterly*, 20, 336–48.

Collier, K.G. (1968) *New Dimensions in Higher Education*. London: Longmans Green.

Collier, K.G. (1969) 'Syndicate methods: further evidence and comment', *Universities Quarterly*, 23, 431–6.

Collier, K.G. (ed.) (1983) *Management of Peer-group Learning: syndicate methods in higher education*. London: Society for Research into Higher Education.

Colman, A.D. (1974) 'Notes on the design process; a psychiatrist looks at architecture', *Journal of Architectural Education*, 27.

Escher, M.C. (1961) *The Graphic Work of M.C. Escher.* London: Oldbourne.

Escher, M.C. (1967) *The Graphic Work of M.C. Escher,* 2nd edn. London: Oldbourne.

Elton, L. and Simmonds, K. (eds) (1977) *Staff Development in Higher Education.* London: Society for Research into Higher Education.

Erskine, C. and Tomkin, A. (1963) 'Evaluation of the effect of the group discussion method in a complex teaching programme', *Journal of Medical Education,* 37, 1036–42.

Foulkes, S.H. (1948) *Introduction to Group Analytic Psychotherapy: studies in the social integration of individuals and groups.* London: Heinemann.

Foulkes, S.H. (1964) *Therapeutic Group Analysis.* London: Allen & Unwin.

Foulkes, S.H. (1975) 'A short outline of the therapeutic processes in group analytic psychotherapy', *Group Analysis,* 8, 1, 60–3.

Foulkes, S.H. and Anthony, E.J. (1957) *Group Psychotherapy.* Harmondsworth: Penguin.

Foulkes, S.H. and Anthony, E.J. (1965) *Group Psychotherapy,* 2nd edn. Harmondsworth: Penguin.

Gibson, E.J. and Walk, R.D. (1960) 'The visual cliff', *Scientific American,* 202, 4, 64–71.

Gibson, J.J. (1950) *The Perception of the Visual World.* Boston: Houghton Mifflin.

Gordon, W.J.J. (1961) *Synectics.* New York: Harper.

Gosling, R., Miller, D.H., Woodhouse, D. and Turquet, P.M. (1967) *The Use of Small Groups in Training.* Hitchin: Codicote Press.

Gregg, A. (1949) 'The Golden Gate of medicine', *Annals of International Medicine,* 30, 810.

Hall, E.T. (1959) *The Silent Language.* New York: Doubleday.

Harlow, H.F. (1959) 'Love in infant monkeys', *Scientific American,* 200, 6, 68–74.

Hazard, J.N. (1962) 'Furniture arrangement as a symbol of judicial roles', *ETC: A Review of General Semantics,* 19, 181–8.

Henry, N.B. (ed.) (1960) 'The dynamics of instructional groups', *59th Year Book of the National Society for the Study of Education, Part II.* Chicago: Chicago University Press.

Ittleson, W. (1952) *The Ames Demonstrations in Perception: a guide to their construction and use.* Princeton, NJ: Princeton University Press.

James, D.W., Johnson, M.L., Venning, P.V. (1956) 'Testing for learnt skill in observation and evaluation of evidence', *Lancet,* ii, 379–83.

Johnson, M.L. (1942) 'Biology and training in observation', *School Science Review,* 92, 56–8.

Johnson, M.L. (1948) 'Biology and training in scientific method', *School Science Review,* 108, 139–47.

Johnson, M.L. (1953a) 'Seeing's believing', in *New Biology* 15. Harmondsworth: Penguin.

Johnson, M.L. (1953b) 'Theory of free group discussion', *Health Education Journal,* ii, 112–17.

Johnson, M.L. and Bauer, M. (1946) 'The scientific value of Higher Certificate Zoology', *School Science Review,* 103, 384–91.

King, M. (1973) 'The anxieties of university teachers', *Universities Quarterly,* 28, 69–83.

Lee, T. (1957) 'On the relations between school journey and social and emotional adjustment in rural infant school children', *British Journal of Educational Psychology,* 27, 101–14.

Lintott, W. and Speirs, R. (1982) 'Cambridge Group Work: a review of its origin and development', *Group Analysis*, 14, 1, 41–6.
McKeachie, W.J. (1963) 'Research on teaching at the college and university level', in Gage, N.L. (ed.) *Handbook of Research on Teaching*. Chicago: Rand McNally.
MacKinnon, D.W. (1962) 'The nature and nurture of creative talent', *American Psychologist*, 17, 484–95.
Morris, B. (1965) 'How does a group learn to work together?', in Niblett, N.R. (ed.) *How and Why Do We Learn?* London: Faber.
National Union of Students (1969) *Report of the Commission on Teaching in Higher Education*. London: NUS.
Nias, J. (1989) *Seeing Anew: teachers' theories of action*. Geelong: Deakin University Press.
Nisbet, S. (1966) 'A method for advanced seminars', *Universities Quarterly*, 20, 349–55.
Osborn, A.F. (1953) *Applied Imagination*. New York: Scribner.
Oxford University (1966) *Commission of Inquiry* (chmn. Baron Franks). *Evidence*. Oxford: Clarendon Press.
Peters, R.J. (1966) *Ethics and Education*. London: Allen & Unwin.
Revans, R. (1964) 'Morale and effectiveness in hospitals', *New Society*, 3, 6–8.
Richardson, E. (1967) *Group Study for Teachers*. London: Routledge.
Royal Institute of British Architects (1969) 'The case for professionalism', *RIBA Journal*, February, 57.
Seguin, C.A. (1965) 'Groups in medical education', *Journal of Medical Education*, 40, 281–5.
Smith, P.B. (1969) *Improving Skills in Working with People: the T-group*. Department of Employment and Productivity Training Information Paper 4. London: HMSO.
Solzhenitsyn, A. (1971) *Cancer Ward*. Harmondsworth: Penguin.
Sommer, R. (1959) 'Studies in personal space', *Sociometry*, 22, 247–60.
Sommer, R. (1969) *Personal Space*. Englewood Cliffs, NJ: Prentice Hall.
Stenhouse, L. (1972) 'Teaching through small group discussion: formality, rules and authority', in Page, C.F. and Greenaway, H. (eds) *Innovation in Higher Education*. London: Society for Research into Higher Education.
University Grants Committee (1964) *Report of the Committee on University Teaching Methods* (Hale Committee). London: HMSO.
Uren, O. (1972) 'Applications of interaction techniques to language teaching', in *Varieties of Group Discussion in University Teaching*. London: University Teaching Methods Unit.
Walton, H.J. (1968) 'An experimental study of different methods for teaching medical students', *Proceedings of the Royal Society of Medicine*, 61, 109–12.
Yalom, I. (1975) *The Theory and Practice of Group Psychotherapy*, 2nd edn. New York: Basic Books.

Index

The Society for Research into Higher Education

The Society for Research into Higher Education exists to stimulate and co-ordinate research into all aspects of higher education. It aims to improve the quality of higher education through the encouragement of debate and publication on issues of policy, on the organization and management of higher education institutions, and on the curriculum and teaching methods.

The Society's income is derived from subscriptions, sales of its books and journals, conference fees and grants. It receives no subsidies, and is wholly independent. Its individual members include teachers, researchers, managers and students. Its corporate members are institutions of higher education, research institutes, professional, industrial and governmental bodies. Members are not only from the UK, but from elsewhere in Europe, from America, Canada and Australasia, and it regards its international work as amongst its most important activities.

Under the imprint *SRHE & Open University Press*, the Society is a specialist publisher of research, having some 45 titles in print. The Editorial Board of the Society's Imprint seeks authoritative research or study in the above fields. It offers competitive royalties, a highly recognizable format in both hardback and paperback and the world-wide reputation of the Open University Press.

The Society also publishes *Studies in Higher Education* (three times a year), which is mainly concerned with academic issues, *Higher Education Quarterly* (formerly *Unversities Quarterly*), mainly concerned with policy issues, *Research into Higher Education Abstracts* (three times a year), and *SRHE News* (four times a year).

The Society holds a major annual conference in December, jointly with an institution of higher education. In 1990, the topic was 'Industry and Higher Education', at and with the University of Surrey. In 1991, it was 'Research and Higher Education in Europe', with the University of Leicester. Conferences have included, in 1992, 'Learning to Effect', with Nottingham Polytechnic, and in 1993, 'Governments and the Higher Education Curriculum' with the University of Sussex. In addition it holds regular seminars and consultations on topics of current interest.

The Society's committees, study groups and branches are run by the members. The groups at present include:

Teacher Education Study Group
Continuing Education Group
Staff Development Group
Excellence in Teaching and Learning
Women in Higher Education Group

Benefits to members

Individual

Individual members receive:

- *SRHE News*, the Society's publications list, conference details and other material included in mailings.
- Greatly reduced rates for *Studies in Higher Education* and *Higher Education Quarterly*.
- A 35% discount on all Open University Press & SRHE publications.
- Free copies of the Precedings – commissioned papers on the theme of the Annual Conference.
- Free copies of *Research into Higher Education Abstracts*.
- Reduced rates for conferences.
- Extensive contacts and scope for facilitating initiatives.
- Reduced reciprocal memberships.

Corporate

Corporate members receive:

- All benefits of individual members, plus
- Free copies of *Studies in Higher Education*.
- Unlimited copies of the Society's publications at reduced rates.
- Special rates for its members e.g. to the Annual Conference.

Membership details: SRHE, 344–354 Gray's Inn Road, London, WC1X 8BP, UK, Tel: 071 837 7880
Catalogue: SRHE & Open University Press, Celtic Court, 22 Ballmoor, Buckingham MK18 1XW. Tel: (0280) 823388

USING EXPERIENCE FOR LEARNING

David Boud, Ruth Cohen and David Walker (eds)

This book is about the struggle to make sense of learning from experience. What are the key ideas that underpin learning from experience? How do we learn from experience? How does context and purpose influence learning? How does experience impact on individual and group learning? How can we help others to learn from their experience?

Using Experience for Learning reflects current interest in the importance of experience in informal and formal learning, whether it be applied for course credit, new forms of learning in the workplace, or acknowledging autonomous learning outside educational institutions. It also emphasizes the role of personal experience in learning: ideas are not separate from experience; relationships and personal interests impact on learning; and emotions have a vital part to play in intellectual learning. All the contributors write themselves into their chapters, giving an autobiographical account of how their experiences have influenced their learning and what has led them to their current views and practice.

Using Experience for Learning brings together a wide range of perspectives and conceptual frameworks with contributors from four continents, and is a valuable addition to the field of experiential learning.

Contents

Contributors
Lee Andresen, David Boud, Angela Brew, Stephen Brookfield, Ruth Cohen, Costas Criticos, Kathleen Dechant, Elizabeth Kasl, Victoria Marsick, John Mason, Nod Miller, John Mulligan, Denis Postle, Mary Thorpe, Robin Usher, David Walker.

208pp   0 335 19095 2 (Paperback)   0 335 19096 0 (Hardback)

HELPING STUDENTS TO LEARN
TEACHING, COUNSELLING, RESEARCH

Kjell Raaheim, Janek Wankowski and John Radford

This is a considerably revised and updated edition of a book first published in 1981. This second edition will be as warmly welcomed as the first:

> This vein of rich and reflective experience runs through the whole book, interspersed with a patterning of psychological theory and educational research findings
> *(Studies in Higher Education)*

> ... it does contain findings which should make all honest academics want to look more closely at their teaching habits and at cherished assumptions about the effectiveness of their contributions. For this reason I should like to see a copy of the book in every university department's library or, better still, in every senior common room
> *(Educational Review)*

> Experience, research and vision blend together ... The book deserves a wide readership, for it is both scholarly and passionate
> *(British Journal of Guidance and Counselling)*

Contents
Teaching and learning: a selective review – From school to university – On the pedagogical skills of university teachers – The need for the development of study skills – The first examinations at university – Success and failure at university – Disenchantment, a syndrome of discontinuity of learning competence – On the vagaries of students' motivations and attitudes to teaching and learning – Assisting the individual student with study difficulties – Reflections and operational prescriptions – Increasing students' power for self-teaching – The teachers and the taught – Bibliography – Name index – Subject index.

192pp   0 335 09319 1 (Paperback)   0 335 09320 5 (Hardback)